NIETZSCHE, PSYCHOLOGY, AND FIRST PHILOSOPHY

ROBERT B. PIPPIN

Nietzsche, Psychology, and First Philosophy

The University of Chicago Press ✳ *Chicago & London*

Originally published in French as Nietzsche, moraliste français
© *Odile Jacob, Février* 2006.
This work is part of the Collège de France *series published by Odile Jacob.*

The University of Chicago Press, Chicago 60637
The University of Chicago Press, Ltd., London
© 2010 by Robert B. Pippin
All rights reserved. Published 2010.
Paperback edition 2011
Printed in the United States of America

20 19 18 17 16 15 14 13 12 11   2 3 4 5 6

ISBN-13: 978-0-226-66975-5 (cloth)
ISBN-13: 978-0-226-66976-2 (paper)
ISBN-10: 0-226-66975-0 (cloth)
ISBN-10: 0-226-66976-9 (paper)

LIBRARY OF CONGRESS CATALOGING-IN-PUBLICATION DATA

Pippin, Robert B., 1948–
Nietzsche, psychology, and first philosophy / Robert B. Pippin.
p. cm.
Includes bibliographical references and index.
ISBN-13: 978-0-226-66975-5 (cloth : alk. paper)
ISBN-10: 0-226-66975-0 (cloth : alk. paper)
1. Nietzsche, Friedrich Wilhelm, 1844–1900—
Criticism and interpretation. I. Title.
B3317.P558 2010
193—dc22

2009034188

In memory of Bernard Williams

Contents

Abbreviations

WORKS BY NIETZSCHE

AC   *Nietzsche: The Anti-Christ, Ecce Homo, Twilight of the Idols, and Other Writings*, ed. Aaron Ridley and Judith Norman (Cambridge: Cambridge University Press, 2005).

BGE   *Beyond Good and Evil*, ed. Rolf-Peter Horstmann and Judith Norman (Cambridge: Cambridge University Press, 2002). (Reference will be to *BGE*, then the paragraph number [§], then the page number—e.g., *BGE*, §29, 30.)

BT   *The Birth of Tragedy*, ed. Raymond Geuss and Ronald Speirs (Cambridge: Cambridge University Press, 1999).

CW   *The Case of Wagner*, in *The Birth of Tragedy and The Case of Wagner*, trans. W. Kaufmann (New York: Vintage, 1967).

D   *Daybreak: Thoughts on the Prejudices of Morality*, ed. Maudemarie Clark and Brian Leiter (Cambridge: Cambridge University Press, 1997).

EH   *Nietzsche: The Anti-Christ, Ecce Homo, Twilight of the Idols, and Other Writings*, ed. Aaron Ridley and Judith Norman (Cambridge: Cambridge University Press, 2005).

GM   *On the Genealogy of Morals*, ed. Keith Ansell Pearson and Carol Diethe (Cambridge: Cambridge University Press, 1994). (Reference will be *GM*, then the essay number [I, II, etc.], then the paragraph number [§], then the page number—e.g., *GM*, I, §9, 16.)

GS   *The Gay Science*, ed. Bernard Williams, trans. J. Nauckhoff and A. Del Caro (Cambridge: Cambridge University Press, 2001). (Reference will be to *GS*, then the paragraph number [§], then the page number—e.g., *GS*, §127, 121–22.)

HAH   *Human, All Too Human: A Book for Free Spirits*, ed. R. J. Hollingdale (Cambridge: Cambridge University Press, 1996).

KSA   *Kritische Studienausgabe*, ed. Gerogio Colli and Mazzino Montinari (Berlin: de Gruyter, 1988).

NF   *Nachgelassene Fragmente*, cited by year, volume number of *KSA*, followed by page number—e.g., *NF* (1883), *KSA*, vol. 10, 243.

NW   *Nietzsche Contra Wagner*, in *EH*.

SE   "Schopenhauer as Educator," in *UM*, cited by *UM* page number.

T   indicates that a translation has been altered.

TI   *Nietzsche: The Anti-Christ, Ecce Homo, Twilight of the Idols, and Other Writings*, ed. Aaron Ridley and Judith Norman (Cambridge: Cambridge University Press, 2005).

TSZ   *Thus Spoke Zarathustra*, ed. Adrian Del Caro and Robert Pippin (Cambridge: Cambridge University Press, 2006).

UM   *Untimely Meditations*, ed. Daniel Breazeale, trans. R. J. Hollingdale (Cambridge.: Cambridge University Press, 1997).

WP   *The Will to Power*, ed. Walter Kaufmann, trans. R. J. Hollingdale (New York: Vintage, 1968).

Acknowledgments

The first four chapters of this book were originally presented in October and November of 2004 as a series of lectures at the Collège de France in Paris and then published as *Nietzsche, moraliste français: La conception nietzschéenne d'une psychologie philosophique* (Paris: Odile Jacob, 2006). I remain very grateful to Marc Fumaroli and Jacques Bouvresse for the invitation to deliver these lectures and for their warm hospitality during my stay in Paris. I remain grateful as well to the Wissenschaftskolleg zu Berlin, where I worked on that version of the lectures in 2003–4 during a research leave there, and to the Andrew W. Mellon Foundation for its Distinguished Achievement Award, which supported much of the research on subsequent additions and revisions.

I have tried out preliminary versions of the interpretations defended here in some earlier articles and lectures, and earlier versions of chapters 5 and 6 were recently published and republished in several edited collections. But I have tried here to present a comprehensive interpretation of what Nietzsche means by "psychology," what the relationship is, as he understands it, between such a psychology and traditional philosophy, and why he thinks such a psychology is (indeed is, as he says, "*now*") so important, why it is "the path to the fundamental problems." In doing so, I have rethought and revised and added substantially to earlier accounts and tried to integrate everything into some sort of whole. I have also tried to attend to the unusual form of Nietzsche's writing and to be sensitive to the way that form makes so difficult (but certainly not impossible) a coherent interpretation of anything like a Nietzschean "position" on anything.

I have been influenced and helped a great deal by many conversations over the past several years with a number of interlocutors, but I am especially grateful to my colleagues and friends here at the University of Chicago, Jonathan Lear and Jim Conant. I have learned more than I can say from their work and from our conversations about Nietzsche over the last decade. Jim Conant also participated, together with Lanier Anderson and Christa Acampora, in an "Author Meets Critics" session on *Nietzsche: moraliste français* organized by the North American Nietzsche Society at the 2007 meetings of the American Philosophical Association, and I was helped immensely in the final revisions of the manuscript by the astute comments of all three critics.

This book is dedicated to the memory of Bernard Williams. His work as a whole, and especially his later work on Nietzsche, remains a great inspiration, as does the vivid memory of his distinctive, elegant, wry, and always thoughtful and original philosophical style.

Introductory Remarks

Many contemporary philosophers want to ask Friedrich Nietzsche questions he himself does not directly address, to make use of what he does say, what he does seem committed to, to try to figure out what he would say, or what he must be committed to, in spite of his silence about various issues, all in a more conventional philosophical language. And there are many who go beyond this "rational reconstruction" way of putting it and insist that Nietzsche is *de dicto*, not just *de re*, committed to a series of conventional philosophical claims in metaphysics and epistemology, however unconventional the content and however oddly dressed up and presented. The topics of most interest in this context are Nietzsche's epistemological perspectivism, his attack on the institution of morality in favor of a naturalistic ethics, and his claims about the will to power, understood either as a general metaphysics or as the major element in a theory of human nature and especially human motivation and basic human drives.

Nietzsche himself, however, constantly raised the issue of how to read and how not to read the philosophical terminology of his work and pointed often to the danger of reading him as though he were a conventional essayist. Indeed, despite the fact that he wrote what seem like essays, he insisted that he did not write essays, that essays "are for asses and journal readers." In many of these metapassages, he insists on what is hidden and unsaid in his writing, that for "aphorism books like mine . . . many lengthy forbidden things and chains of thought stand between and behind short aphorisms" (*KSA*, vol. 7, 3, 37 [June–July 1885]). He writes, he says, as a hermit in a cave, "whose very concepts finally retain a peculiar twilight color, a smell as much of the depths as mold, something incommunicable and reluctant which blows coldly upon all the merely curious." "A hermit's philosophy," he writes, "even if it were written with a lion's claw [*wenn sie selbst mit einer Löwen Klaue geschrieben wäre*] would still only look like a philosophy of goose feet, a philosophy of question marks [*eine Philosophie der Gansfüschen*]."[1] In *Beyond Good and Evil*, he even tells us that "One no longer loves one's knowledge enough as soon as one communicates it" (*BGE*, §160, 71). Given such claims, there are even occasional attempts to develop an esoteric reading of Nietzsche, but by and large his frequent warnings that almost everything of importance in his writing is unsaid, ironic, or "in question marks" have received little notice.

These remarks and many other warnings are mostly just that, warnings, and they are quite vague, prompting the understandable attempt at more conventional restatements. I take my bearings in the following from the interesting point once made by Bernard Williams: that both Ludwig Wittgenstein and Nietzsche were trying to say something about what it might mean for philosophy itself to come to an end, for a culture to be "cured" of philosophy. He meant the end of philosophical theory, the idea that unaided human reason could contribute to knowledge about substance, being, our conceptual scheme, the highest values, the meaning of history, or the way language works. For both Wittgenstein and Nietzsche, there is no good or modest version of these attempts any more than there are good and bad versions of astrology or alchemy. There is no such thing as philosophical theory, and there never was.[2] Of course it has always been obvious that the

---

1. See Heftrich 1962 (5ff), which cites these notes.

2. Although there could, paradoxically, still be philosophers. In Giorgio Colli's apt formulation, "Die Philosophie existiert nicht mehr, aber die Philosophen müssen weiter existieren [Philosophy no longer exists, but philosophers must continue to]" (*KSA*, vol. 3, 661).

status of the account that somehow *makes* this observation is immediately problematic, but Williams also noted that the case of Nietzsche was even more difficult than that of Wittgenstein. "With Nietzsche, by contrast, the resistance to the continuation of philosophy by ordinary means is built into the text, which is booby-trapped, not only against recovering theory from it, but, in many cases, against any systematic exegesis that assimilates it to theory."[3] Now, as far as I know, in the long history of rhetoric, there is no commonly agreed on definition of what a textual "booby trap" might be, but it is probably a British way of pointing at something similar to what many influential French commentators such as Paul de Man, Giles Deleuze, Sarah Kofman, and Jacques Derrida have said, that Nietzsche's texts always seem to take away with one hand what they appear to have given with the other. Depending on your point of view, one might say either that, despite appearances, Nietzsche does not intend to offer philosophical theories about anything, or that he somehow enacts more unwittingly the impossibility of any such theory, or even the impossibility of textual coherence and referentiality. At any rate, the important point is not his resistance to incorporation into traditional philosophical theory. That point is obvious, even if the steady stream of books about Nietzsche's metaphysics, or value theory, or even epistemology shows no sign of abating. The interesting question is rather what one takes such resistance to mean, what the practical point is, we might say, of the act of so resisting, what Nietzsche is trying to *do* with his books, as much as what his books mean, if we are not to understand them in the traditional philosophical sense. (It would have been helpful if, in *Ecce Homo*, Nietzsche had not just written the chapter "Why I Write Such Good Books" but "Why I Write Books at All.")

The fact that Nietzsche might be doing something different from offering philosophical theories need not of course at all imply that he is not doing *anything*, or not doing anything of any relevance *to* philosophy, or that he is enacting the impossibility of making *any* sort of point against others. (Noting this already marks the beginning of a difference, at least in principle, between what Williams is suggesting about Nietzsche and the contemporary French reading.) This is a tricky issue, for it involves two of Nietzsche's most interesting and

3. Bernard Williams 1994, 238.

vastly ambitious ideas. One is that a certain form of life, a commitment to values stemming from Greek rationalism and Christianity ("Platonism for the people") is coming to an end, or "dying." By and large he means that such values have ceased to be useful for "life" (although they used to be), but the question of how and why a form of life might be said to die out is worth several books in itself.[4] His second grand claim is interwoven with the first and has to do with what he called the "value of truth." There has been much paradox mongering around this issue in Nietzsche, but he seems most interested in the discovery not that truth in the Platonic sense is simply impossible (although he was obviously occasionally tempted to make such claims) but that we have come to see that it does not, cannot, do for us what our hopes had held out.[5] But for the moment we must begin much more simply by letting Nietzsche help us understand what *he* thinks he is up to. We can then see immediately why even his own main category, which I claim in this book is "psychology," is so rhetorically complicated and elusive.

I do not pretend that this last is an easy question to formulate, and it will take me most of the rest of this book to try to make clearer how I think Nietzsche wanted to raise that issue. In chapter 1, I want to look at how Nietzsche understands the project of psychology as something like "first philosophy"; in chapter 2, what, according to Nietzsche, makes a science a "gay" science and how such a science understands the difference between a living and a dead value; in chapter 3, how the announcement of the "death of God" in *The Gay Science* (§125) changes (or not) the prospects for such a gay science; and in chapter 4, I want to explore the implications of the way Nietzsche is treating these questions for the basic notions of action, agent, and responsibility, as these are laid out in yet another famous image in *On the Genealogy of Morals*.

4. This is especially so because Nietzsche's claim about the irrelevance of modern science and philosophy for life (for guiding a life) was so extraordinarily influential (Max Weber's "Science as Vocation" essay is only one of many examples; the implications of the fact for Carl Schmitt would be another) and because of the way the situation provoked so many *Lebensphilosophien* ("philosophies of life") as correctives of a sort to this "crisis," Martin Heidegger's being the most well known. For more on how Nietzsche understands the relation between practical commitments and theoretical truth, see Poellner 2009.

5. I defend this reading in "Truth and Lies in the Early Nietzsche" (Pippin 1997, 311–29).

The last two chapters will explore the implications of this account for what might be called Nietzschean "freedom."

In effect, what I am primarily interested in are four Nietzschean figurative claims or images—that truth could be a woman, that a science could be gay, that God could die, and that there is no "lightning" separate from its "flash"—and why it is a set of literary tropes that carry so much of the freight. These are then taken to have implications for two issues of central concern for Nietzsche: self-deceit and "self-overcoming," topics that themselves almost require images and metaphors to be stated properly: that one can "hide" from oneself and that one can "overcome" oneself.

CHAPTER ONE

Psychology as "the Queen of the Sciences"

I.

In paragraph 23 of *Beyond Good and Evil*, Nietzsche encourages us to "clench your teeth! open your eyes! and grab hold of the helm!" We are to make a voyage that will entitle us to demand that "psychology again be recognized as the queen of the sciences, and that the rest of the sciences exist to serve and prepare for it. Because, from now on, psychology is again the path to the most fundamental problems" (*BGE*, §23, 24).

This seems to state very clearly that Nietzsche, by mentioning the "*queen* of the sciences" and "*fundamental* problems," is claiming that "psychology" as he understands it will replace philosophy, especially metaphysics, the former and presumably dead or deposed queen. (To be sure, there is in the passage a distinction between the "path" to the problems, which path is psychology, and the "fundamental problems" themselves, the precise character of which is unnamed. But this appears to be a distinction between what psychology will explain and the basic explicanda, the problems of value at the heart of Nietzsche's interests. Or so I shall argue below.)

What could this mean? What could "psychology" in that claim refer to, and why would it not be just one of the sciences but their "queen"? If this is not an empirical psychology, is it a "philosophical psychology"? What would its object be? The soul? What does Nietzsche mean by "again"? *When* was psychology like first philosophy? How does all this square with Nietzsche's resistance to "theory"? My thesis in this book is that, however resistant he may be to philosophical theory, Nietzsche's claim here is a serious one and has a determinate content (his "booby traps" are not self-immolating; something is left standing) and that we have not yet understood either that content or in what sense Nietzschean psychology might replace, even serve as the explicans for, metaphysics or first philosophy in any sense.[1]

There are some general characteristics of a Nietzschean psychology with which most Nietzsche commentators would agree. First, he is primarily interested in what we need to say about the psyche to understand what happens when we act on the basis of some value claim or express in some way a commitment to a value. (One way of interpreting Nietzsche on the priority of psychology is already visible: he clearly believes that *any* activity, whether theoretical or practical, already involves such a commitment, and so the place of value and its psychological conditions in the economy of the soul must be "fundamental" for any other activity.)[2] Academic philosophy now characterizes this set of concerns—as they appear in Plato and Aristotle, through David Hume, to Elizabeth Anscombe and Donald Davidson—as "moral psychology," or "philosophical psychology." Typical questions include: What is the relation between reason and the passions in action? Can reason alone direct action? Is akrasia, or knowing the better but doing the worse, possible? And so forth. As we have already seen, however, Nietzsche does not appear to want simply to add another position to this list. Indeed, his main point seems to be that there is no general *philosophical* psychology. His view, which I will be exploring in these chapters,

1. Both of the questions noted above—what it means for a form of life to die out and what Nietzsche means by the declining "value" of truth—are already examples of how accepting the priority of psychology changes the way we ask questions of Nietzsche. On the former issue, see the invaluable study by Jonathan Lear (2006).

2. Echoing Goethe, Nietzsche insists in *GM*, I, §13, 26, that "Das Thun ist alles [The doing is everything]." I discuss the implications of this turn of phrase in chapter 4.

is that views of the soul and its capacities vary with beliefs about and commitments to norms; normative commitments are subject to radical historical change; and so what counts as soul or psyche or mind and thus psychology also changes. The "soul" is merely the name for a collective historical achievement, a mode of self-understanding, of one sort or another, what we have made ourselves into at one point or other in the service of some ideal or other. When we describe to one another what we think the soul is, we mean thereby to propose an ideal, usually something like psychic health. Hence also the deep interconnection or inseparability between psychology and genealogy. This is a point that will emerge frequently throughout what follows.[3]

Second, it is often said that Nietzschean psychology must be "naturalist," and third, that it is therefore largely deflationary. The former, "naturalism," requirement amounts to an insistence that, when trying to account for the human capacities required when persons direct their actions on the basis of norms, we should appeal to capacities also discoverable in nonmoral or nonethical contexts, and those capacities must be consistent with our being organic material bodies located in space and time. If we can only explain normative constraints and a set of practices by appealing to a capacity uniquely required by a particular view of value (such as a free will, an uncaused cause, or a unified subject independent of and directing its deeds), especially if that capacity is supranatural, the odds are high, at the very least, that we are dealing with a kind of philosophical fantasy.[4]

This enterprise turns out to be critical and deflationary, especially with regard to the set of values and practices that Nietzsche designates as "morality"—the Christian and post-Christian values of universal

3. As Zarathustra says, living is leading or directing a life, and so living essentially *is* esteeming (*Schätzen*) or valuing. So the priority of psychology looks very like Nietzsche's occasional suggestion that all human phenomena, including knowledge claims, be looked at "from the perspective of life." Psychology, that is, will make manifest what is involved, what we are committed to, in understanding "living" in this sense. As has already been noted, from the time of the second *Untimely Meditation* on, Nietzsche claimed that modern philosophy and science and religion and even art had lost any connection with life in this sense, and insofar as any of these enterprises had a living presence in modern culture, they were actively life-denying presences.

4. This is how Bernard Williams (1994) encourages us to understand what he calls Nietzsche's "minimalist psychology."

equality, absolute individual responsibility, and guilt. The way the psyche "works" in commitment to and pursuit of moral values is in reality[5] far different from the self-descriptions of moral agents. (That psychology is the sort of fantasy just described.)

Finally, though, if the Nietzschean enterprise is deflationary, it is not reductionist. One of the things natural organic beings can do, must do, is to create all sorts of different institutions under varying circumstances, train themselves to observe certain constraints and not others, and there is no reason to believe that exclusive attention to the biological or physical properties or evolutionary histories of these organisms best explains (or could explain at all) why they create one sort rather than another, nor is there any way a purely natural science account could explain what these institutions actually mean to the participants, what they take themselves to be doing.

II.

But why should psychology, understood in this way, be so important that it becomes "the *queen* of the sciences" and thus functions like metaphysics used to function, as the path to all the *"fundamental problems"*?

Here is a conventional view, one with which we are all familiar. Nietzsche seems to be referring to a new sort of fundamental doctrine or teaching, let us say—perhaps an aesthetic picture or perhaps a legislation of a new value—that takes in "everything," as much cosmology as ontology, as much metaphysics as natural science. The "will to power" seems to be the name of this new doctrine, and such a doctrine clearly has many psychological implications. All of nature, especially organic nature, most especially human psychological nature, is to be understood as the expression of a basic drive to dominate and exert

---

5. I mean in *historical* reality. The real roles of ressentiment, hatred, and revenge are not instances of any general law about the psyche but aspects of a slavish institution at a time. To deny that this restriction to historical time could be a possible explanation (because linked to something historically unique) is like saying we cannot discuss why Emma Bovary had an affair with Leon unless we see it as an instance of a general law about bored provincial housewives.

power over as much as possible, not to be subject to any other will or drive. This almost seems to amount to a psychologizing of being itself, attributing to everything what seems in itself a psychological drive.[6] After all, paragraph 23 in *Beyond Good and Evil* had begun with "All psychology so far has been stuck in moral prejudices and fears: it has not ventured into the depths. To grasp psychology as morphology and *the doctrine of the development of the will to power*, which is what I have done—nobody has ever come close to this, not even in thought" (*BGE*, §23, 23).

Nietzsche is famous for having said such things as "Life itself is will to power" (*BGE*, §13, 15),[7] and a bit later in his *Genealogy*, he had written "that everything that occurs in the organic world consists of *overpowering, dominating,* and, in their turn, overpowering and dominating consist of re-interpretation, adjustment" (*GM*, II, §12, 51). And, in a much-quoted passage in the same section, "But every purpose and use is just a *sign* that the will to power has achieved mastery over something less powerful, and has impressed upon it its own idea [*Sinn*] of a use function; and the whole history of a 'thing,' an organ, a tradition can to this extent be a continuous chain of signs, continually revealing new interpretations and adaptations" (*GM*, II, §12, 51).

These are standard quotations, although there are indications immediately that it will not be easy to find the right category for these claims. For one thing, even though Nietzsche seems to be talking about the organic world here, this "dominating [*Herrwerden*]" is, rather oddly, discussed in terms of "new interpretations [*Neu-Interpretieren*]" and "adaptations [*ein Zurechtmachen*]." This sounds like some *gigantomachia* of philologists, not the sort of bloody test of brute, cruel, merciless strength with which Nietzsche has been associated. The same is true of

6. For a standard statement of this position, see Kaufmann 1968 (206-7).

7. Perhaps the most famous passage is *BGE*, §36. As Maudmarie Clark has pointed out, this famous claim that the world "von innen gesehen [seen from inside]," with respect to its "intelligibilen Charakter [intelligible character]," would be "Wille zur Macht und nichts außerdem ['will to power' and nothing else]" is stated as a conditional and relies on premises (like the causality of will itself) that Nietzsche elsewhere explicitly rejects (*BGE*, §36, 35-36). I would add that the idea of the "intelligible character" of the world is in scare quotes because it also invokes a premise that Nietzsche clearly denies. Clark is also right to note the nearby passage on exoteric and esoteric meanings. See Clark's essay (1983, especially 464-65).

phrases like "a continuous chain of signs of ever new interpretations and adaptations." Nietzsche clearly does not want "power" to function as a purpose or basic drive, since he is admitting freely that what *counts* as power changes frequently and radically and so itself is a subject of contestation and dispute. (Unless power were a very un-Nietzschean end in itself, it is also unclear how the appeal to power would figure in any psychological explanation, since it is unlikely that persons would *simply* seek to gain power unless they already desired some end that such power could serve.)[8] Moreover, unless we are willing to think that Nietzsche actually believed that the cosmos was some sort of living brute with its own psychology, this sort of approach leaves us right back again with metaphysical foundations and psychological implications, exactly the model Nietzsche says he is replacing.[9]

For another thing, it is easy here to explode one of the "booby traps" planted by Nietzsche. Here is one from the "Assorted Opinions and Maxims" section of *Human, All Too Human*. (It contains the hint or clue that I will follow through these chapters, so I will quote it at length.) "An original sin of philosophers.—Philosophers have at all times appropriated the propositions of the examiners of men (moralists) and *ruined* them, inasmuch as they have taken them for unqualified propositions and sought to demonstrate the absolute validity of what these moralists intended merely as approximate signposts or

8. And there is no indication that Nietzsche either thinks that we can simply will to have desires that can be satisfied effectively or that he thinks *all* desires are in fact desires for power (in which case the will to power could be distinguished from nothing else and would explain nothing, as Clark [1983] points out).

9. The attack on any putative autonomy or priority for philosophy in the name of psychology can get quickly complicated in the passages where Nietzsche discusses it, since the nature of any appeal to psychological factors is itself characterized as his own strategy of sorts, already a contestation over kinds of lives and evaluations of such kinds. This can make for very compressed passages and confusing implications. In BGE, the "conscious thought" of a philosopher is said to be "directed and forced into certain channels by his instincts," but the psychological reductionism suggested is then undercut by the fact that these instincts are identified not with impulses or passions but with "valuations [*Wertschätzungen*]," a qualification itself complicated when these valuations themselves are then redescribed as "physiological," although, to complete the circle again, not physiological forces but demands (*Forderungen*) for the "preservation of a particular type of life" (*BGE*, §3, 7). (There are few passages as representative of the denseness and complexity of Nietzsche's style.)

even as no more than truths possessing tenancy only for a decade—and through doing so thought to elevate themselves above the latter" (*HAH*, 215). The example Nietzsche gives of this original sin is a telling one— Arthur Schopenhauer on the will. Nietzsche claims that Schopenhauer was in reality, without appreciating the fact himself, a "moralist," who rightly used the term *will* loosely and "remoulded as a common designation for many different human states and inserted a gap in the language" and so earned the right "to speak of the 'will' as Blaise Pascal had spoken of it." Unfortunately, though, "the philosopher's rage for generalization" turned such a moralist *façon de parler* into a metaphysical claim about the omnipresence of the will in all of nature (a claim Nietzsche calls a piece of "mystical mischief [*mystische Unfuge*]") and so ended up turning everything "towards a false reification [*zu einer falschen Verdinglichung*]."[10]

I would venture to guess that if the "Nietzsche community" were to agree that no new book on Nietzsche could be written until it was made consistent with this admonition, publication would grind virtually to a halt. What Nietzsche is warning against here—the substantialization and reification of what is really a kind of placeholder used to very different purposes by "moralists"—is an interpretive tendency shared both by the anglophone academic philosophy literature and the European literature so influenced by Heidegger's lectures on Nietzsche in the 1930s, which famously claimed Nietzsche as a metaphysical thinker and the will to power as his metaphysical doctrine.[11]

Even more valuable is the reference to "examiners of men [*Menschenprüfer*]," or to "the moralists." To whom is he referring? Explicitly and quite favorably in this passage to Pascal. Now it is always acknowledged that the great "French moralists," especially but not exclusively of the sixteenth and seventeenth centuries, were heroes to Nietzsche,

---

10. Nietzsche makes the same charge against Schopenhauer in *GS*, §127, 121–22. Pascal is the French *moraliste* mentioned here, but Jessica Berry has shown the great importance of Montaigne as well in Nietzsche's break with Schopenhauer in *HAH*. See Berry 2004.

11. In his first 1936 lectures on Nietzsche, Heidegger says that Nietzsche's basic thought is "the will to power," that it is an "answer to the question, 'what is it to be an entity,'" and so is a "metaphysical" doctrine, a "name for the basic character [*Grundcharakter*] of any entity [*Seiende*]" (Heidegger 1961, 1:12). The passage is entitled "Nietzsche als metaphysischer Denker [Nietzsche as Metaphysical Thinker]."

that he mentions them often and often with exorbitant praise.[12] It is also clear that he treats them as "psychologists" in a very broad sense but with that specific focus noted above—how we should understand what happens when people appeal to normative considerations, or try to live well, how those norms have come to matter to people, how even they could or could not come to matter.

The names in question are also clear: above all and by a wide margin, Michel Montaigne (about whom he had almost nothing critical to say)[13] and also François La Rochefoucauld and Pascal round out the top and pretty distinct group.[14] These three especially all join a Nietzschean pantheon with very few members: the pre-Socratics, Greek poets, some Romans, a few from the Italian Renaissance, Napoleon, Goethe, and Shakespeare. He even once dedicated a whole book to Voltaire (although he eventually lost faith in Voltaire's optimism and reliance on reason),[15] and Stendhal is also frequently lionized, again

---

12. A typical summary from *Ecce Homo*: "I basically keep coming back to a small number of old Frenchmen: I only believe in French culture and I consider everything else that gets called 'culture' in Europe to be a misunderstanding; I won't even mention German culture" (*EH*, 90). It is interesting that Nietzsche relied heavily on Albert Lang's *Geschichte des Materialismus* (*History of Materialism*), read most of the French in German translation, but often cited the works in French. See Molner 1993 and Williams 1952.

13. Perhaps the clearest and most enthusiastic about Montaigne: "I know of only one writer whom I would compare with Schopenhauer, indeed set above him, in respect of honesty: Montaigne. That such a man wrote has truly augmented the joy of living on this earth. Since getting to know this freest and mightiest of souls, I at least have come to feel what he felt about Plutarch: 'as soon as I glance in him I grow a leg or a wing.' If I were set the task, I would endeavor to make myself at home in the world with him" (*UM*, 135). As we shall see soon, the Platonic, Phaedrus-like sexual imagery at the end of this passage is no accident. For some mild criticism of Montaigne (on skepticism), see *BGE*, §101, 208. See Berry 2004 for a valuable account of Montaigne's "An Apology for Raymond Sebond" essay and the related development of Nietzsche's own understanding of "naturalism" (and its relation to skepticism). Berry's account of Nietzsche's *HAH* analysis of "science" as "moral psychology" is especially important.

14. There are in the *KSA* a total of forty-eight references for Montaigne, ninety-eight for Pascal, and twenty-seven for La Rochefoucauld. Given what Nietzsche felt about Benedict de Spinoza, it is extraordinary praise for Nietzsche to say that Pascal "ist tiefer als Spinoza [is deeper than Spinoza]" (*KSA*, vol. II, 563).

15. Cf. *GS*, §37, 55.

as a "moralist." It is sometimes said that this French influence is only relevant to Nietzsche's own "moraliste" period, or the three books *Human, All Too Human*, *Daybreak*, and *The Gay Science*,[16] but as we have already seen, the formulations of his task as "psychology" extend well beyond this period. We will see their influence in *Beyond Good and Evil*, *On the Genealogy of Morals*, and his autobiography of sorts, *Ecce Homo*.[17]

There are others (Nicolas Chamfort, Paul Bourget, Vauvenargue [Luc de Clapiers], even some interesting remarks about Bernard de Fontenelle),[18] but what is important, I propose, is the direction suggested by the passage just quoted from *Human, All Too Human*. I can state the thesis that I want to argue very simply in the terms of that passage: Nietzsche is much better understood not as a great German metaphysician, or as the last metaphysican of the West, or as the destroyer or culminator of metaphysics, or as very interested in metaphysics or a new theory of nature at all, but as one of the great "French moralists." The point is not only that that is how he sees himself but that this is what he is trying "to do" with his work, as I put it before, and it is much more interesting, provokes more interesting questions and counters than he does "qua metaphysician." The questions are clear: what *sort* of a psychologist is a "moraliste"?[19] But more problematically: in what way does such a psychologist avoid the "original sin" of philosophy, the "false reification [*falsche Verdinglichung*]" of his terms of explanation so typical of philosophers? And, yet again, in what sense is such an enterprise the queen of the sciences?

16. Cf. Donnellan 1982. Cf. also Nietzsche's summary account of French superiority, their "voluptate psychologica" in *BGE*, §254, 145-47.

17. Brobjer has made by far (to say the least) the most detailed study of Nietzsche's reading habits and the authors who influenced him throughout his life and is able to show the broad extent of Montaigne's influence, especially during the crucial years 1883-85. See Brobjer 2008, 90.

18. For Nietzsche's lists of the worthy French, see *HAH*, 362; *NF* (1883); *KSA*, vol. 10, 243; for the famous descent into Hades passage, pairing Epicurus with Montaigne, Goethe with Spinoza, Plato with Rousseau, and Pascal with Schopenhauer, see *HAH*, 299.

19. "A normative psychologist everywhere informed by genealogy" I have suggested in a preliminary way, although that could mean any number of things at this point.

III.

What interests Nietzsche in "essays" or "maxims" or "pensées," I want to suggest, is that they are presented without, and with no hidden reliance on, a "deeper" philosophical theory of human nature or of reason or of anything else, and it is clearly an assumption in all three (and by Nietzsche) that this is not a limitation but unavoidable if one is to write "honestly," and so is a virtue. Pascal's "*l'homme honnête*" is the clear model for the Nietzschean "free spirit [*freie Geist*]" from the 1876 *Nachlass* written in preparation for *Human, All Too Human* and thereafter.[20] It is also no accident that the three moralists Nietzsche admired the most wrote in such unusual, original forms, as we shall see.[21]

Here is what I think Nietzsche got from this reading of *les moralistes*, especially in the late 1870s, although it carried over into all his mature works: while, according to Nietzsche, La Rochefoucauld's tendency to see petty egoism everywhere finally belittles man unfairly, and while Pascal's noble soul was eventually crushed by Christianity or the Christian understanding of the weakness and depravity of man, the Nietzschean question is at its clearest with Montaigne. *How*, he wants to know above all, did Montaigne manage to exhibit such a thoroughgoing skepticism and clarity about human frailty and failings *without* Pascal's despair and eventual surrender[22] or La Rochefoucauld's icy contempt for the "human all too human"?[23] Instead, Montaigne ended up a thoughtful, ferociously honest, cheerful free spirit, someone who

20. Vivarelli (1994) has established this convincingly. Cf. also *HAH*, §50, 38–39, for Nietzsche and La Rochefoucauld on pity. For criticisms of La Rochefoucauld as still bound to essentially Christian categories of evaluation, see *NF* (1880–81); *KSA*, vol. 9, 295; *NF* (1881–82); and *KSA*, vol. 9, 441.

21. One might say of Nietzsche what Floyd Gray said of Montaigne: "On peut dire que c'est le mot même qui fait sortir de la plume de l'écrivain tout un nouveau monde, toute une association d'idées qui n'existerait pas avant . . . les mots ne sont-ils pas appelés par le mouvement automatique de l'esprit de Montaigne plutôt que par le sens?" (Gray 1958, 9). See also Molner 1993, 87.

22. For more passages on "the Pascal problem," see *UM*, 135. *BGE*, §62, 57 enlists Pascal in Nietzsche's own view of Christian degeneracy, and there are Pensées that could have been written by Nietzsche (the famous "Le moi est haïssable" paragraph) and Pascal's remarks about the two qualities of the self (Pascal 1963, 584).

23. Cf. *HAH*, §36.

had succeeded at the task of "making [himself] at home in the world [*sich auf der Erde heimisch zu machen*]."[24]

When the question is formulated this way, it is clear that what Nietzsche is looking for is not, cannot be, an argument in Montaigne that could demonstrate or justify his overall stance toward the human world, his basic mode of being-in-the-world one might say with Heidegger. (As with Heidegger, so for Nietzsche, being-in-the-world must be actively sustained in some way, as in the sustaining of commitments and projects. Heidegger's term for such a possibility is *Sorge*, "care," a term with connections to many of the themes in Nietzsche introduced below. Nietzsche is especially interested in questions similar to those posed by the early Heidegger, such as, Under what conditions is such concern or care or eros, our orienting commitments, let us say, sustainable, and how could it (i.e., such a way of "mattering") come to fail? What *is* such mattering that it could fail? In Montaigne's case, Nietzsche realizes that there is no theory underlying the *way* the world matters to him, as if there were an implied theory about how things could matter and the world fulfills enough of the requirements. All such approaches to Montaigne would be wrong, would simply miss the whole point of Montaigne. What Montaigne understood, how he understood it, what we would be misunderstanding if, with our "reifying" tendencies, we asked for his "theory of what matters, of significance, of human nature," and so forth, where and why we would be going wrong in asking such questions, is what Nietzsche is after, what he is pointing to with that distinction between how a *moraliste* or an examiner of men (*Menschenprüfer*) thinks and writes, and the way a philosopher or metaphysician does.

Now, a brief qualification is necessary here. This desideratum represents a "Montaigne-inspired *ideal*" for Nietzsche. He clearly never succeeded in reaching it. The fact that his prose sometimes lapsed into a shrieking intensity, the occasional hysteria, the drift into the maudlin and the sentimental, the hatred venting through some passages, do not at all evince a Montaigne-like peace of mind. Zarathustra may

---

24. *UM*, 135. See also *HAH*, 36 on Le Rochefoucauld and the "danger" that Montaigne avoided. *HAH*, 32. Also, *D*, 46: "Doubt upon doubt.—'What a fine pillow doubt is for a well-made head!' This word of Montaigne's always embittered Pascal, for no one demanded so heftily for a good pillow as he. What is lacking here?"

have been cured of his "illness," his despair about mankind, but it is not at all clear that Nietzsche ever was, and it would be an interesting but independent question to pursue the implications of that failure, especially since I believe Nietzsche was well aware of it.

But with these two issues, we are back to our original questions, but now with more signposts. Nietzsche's psychological account will not be philosophical theory, in the same way that Montaigne's essays can be said to make determinate claims without being philosophy, and it will not be second-rate or merely "popular philosophy," not quite up to the standards of rigor in real philosophy. And the key to why such a psychology will be a sort of replacement for first philosophy will be the primacy of the "psychological" question of some basic, always presupposed "stance toward life," an orientation such that things in a life matter or they don't. (The question of Montaigne's equanimity, his "cheerfulness [*Heiterkeit*]," is not in the usual sense just a psychological or an autobiographical matter because it is implicated in the "fate of value" question. In fact, being able to will, in the general sense of affirm, direct a life in a way that evinces a sustainable, "living" commitment, amounts to the realization of the will to power in the sense in which Nietzsche most uses it. And, as Zarathustra seems to realize, one cannot achieve such a state alone.)[25] This is a stance or an orientation that cannot be addressed by argument or systematic philosophy or revelation, or at least not by any of them alone, because that would already assume the preeminent importance of argument or system or revelation.

There are indications of what is most at stake for Nietzsche in these questions in the very beginning passages of his three most famous books, *Thus Spoke Zarathustra*, *On the Genealogy of Morals*, and *Beyond Good and Evil*. The last is especially famous, and I will pursue the psychology question by closing with a discussion of it in this chapter.

IV.

First, consider the opening passages. *Thus Spoke Zarathustra* begins with Zarathustra addressing the sun from his cave (the Platonic

---

25. Cf. the interpretation of this fact in Pippin 1988 and its implications for Zarathustra's unique rhetoric in Pippin 2006.

resonances are not accidental, as we shall see) and deciding—again, like Socrates in the *Republic*—to "go down" or "go under." We are given no real explanation for the decision, but Zarathustra meets a hermit who asks him why he is returning. Zarathustra's answer (one that is almost completely neglected in commentaries) is simply, "I love mankind" (*TSZ*, 4). At the beginning of *On the Genealogy of Morals*, a similar sort of issue—the issue of eros, let us say—is raised. After Nietzsche had declared that we do not know ourselves because we have never sought ourselves, he quotes a passage from Matthew's gospel: "Where your treasure is, there will your heart be also" (*GM*, preface, §1, 3). Our treasure (we moderns) is, he says, hope for knowledge, for the transformative and redemptive power of knowing itself. But what is important in the passage is the claim for priority of some sort of erotic striving, a matter of the heart (an image that resonates with Pascal's famous "Le coeur a ses raisons, que la raison ne connaît point").[26]

The most famous and disputed invocation of erotic imagery, though, occurs in the first lines of *Beyond Good and Evil*.[27] The image brings together all at once the priority of the psychology theme, the centrality of eros in that claim, the insufficiency of philosophy, and the need to write differently once such an insufficiency is realized. "Suppose that truth is a woman—and why not? Aren't there reasons for suspecting that all philosophers, to the extent that they have been dogmatists, have not really understood women? That the grotesque seriousness of their approach towards the truth and the clumsy advances they have made so far are unsuitable ways of pressing their suit with a woman?" (*BGE*, preface, 3). So, philosophers are like lovers, suitors; or, as he says more often in other passages, seducers. More to the point, philosophers should be understood as inexpert, clumsy lovers.

26. Pascal 1963, §423, 552.

27. I go over here material also covered and discussed at much greater length in chapter 14 of Pippin 1997 (358ff.). The larger issue concerns what it means for Nietzsche to assert that in his approach, "life" is the most comprehensive perspective, something even like a condition for the possibility of knowledge claims and moral evaluation. On a straightforward reading, this seems to mean that everything, including science and morality, is to be relativized to this perspective, as if we should come to believe only what is "useful" for life. And this looks like an appeal to wishful thinking, or a confusion of psychological with philosophical issues. I argue in this chapter that such inferences are based on misinterpretations of the basic claim about life.

Philosophers, or those committed to truth and some hope of moral objectivity, want something out of existence, believe that sustaining their commitments and pursuing their projects are possible only if one knows what is truly worth pursuing, and they desire ardently to know that, to succeed. By couching his description of philosophy in erotic terms, Nietzsche is already suggesting several aspects of what he says elsewhere. First, this implies (to him) a few/many distinction. Not everyone can be expected to be seized by such a desire for this unconditional assurance about the ultimate justifiability of one's projects; and, second, he is emphasizing again the "priority of the psychological." The natural object of eros is, let us say, the beautiful, and so the question of who does or does not find a philosophical life in this sense beautiful, more beautiful than any other, cannot be the result of any demonstration. Someone cannot be argued into desiring this sort of beauty, argued away from what she might find more beautiful, for example, a pious life or a socially useful life. What most matters is what inspires some great erotic striving, and what most matters to us is in an odd way quite "independent" of us, "always already there," to invoke another Heideggerean turn of phrase.

But the central point of the image is that philosophers go about satisfying this desire inexpertly and clumsily, with amateurish expectations. Presumably, if we understand this, we can also understand something of Nietzsche's own account of what it means to be "attached," bound or committed to one's perspective or way of life, what it means to be able to limit and discipline oneself (or one's culture) in the service of some loved end, and all perhaps, finally, in the manner of Montaigne, without overly optimistic, ultimately self-defeating, philosophic hopes, and without the despair of Pascal or the cynicism of La Rochefoucauld.

Now, the standard way of understanding this passage is by portraying Nietzsche as a sophist in the Protagorean sense and by appealing to Nietzsche's crude, often simply misogynist use of women in his metaphors and similes. What philosophers really want, supposedly, is a kind of power over the views and activities of others (the way a seducer wants a kind of victory over someone). The "truth" that they love can only really be a kind of success in such persuasion, to be able to subject others to the way one wants things seen, not to be subjected. (Socrates was not "the beginning of the Greek enlightenment";

he simply persuaded people to fight using weapons with which he was sure to win.) Women are the experts in appearance, illusion, and the manipulation of desire. Philosophers love this rhetorical success at such manipulation, but, what with their arguments, debating techniques, and self-importance, they are clumsy at achieving it when compared with real experts, women. Rather, as in the famous epigram from Zarathustra that begins the third essay in *On the Genealogy of Morals*, "Carefree, mocking, violent—this is how wisdom wants *us*: she is a woman, all she ever loves is a warrior" (*GM*, III, §1, 68). I suppose the lesson of the conventional reading is that just as women love only "real men" or warriors, philosophical truth or wisdom is a manly thing, a matter of active, powerful legislation, not supplication or "feminine" passivity.

V.

This conventional view is not so much wrong, I want now to suggest, as quite incomplete and so very misleading. In the first place, we should note that the psychology of love is a useful and broad window onto Nietzsche's psychological analysis of the philosophical type. This is so because most of us do not think of erotic attachments to other people as simply caused by psychological impulses; we think of such attachments as expressive, revelations of the more important and worthy aspects of ourselves, and so as also partly evaluative, at least in this expressive sense. (Those whom we love must be lovable in some sense.) But we also do not think of such attachments as the product of deliberation and normative evaluation, as if consequent upon some mere list of worthy and unworthy qualities. So the suggestion of the passage seems to be: think of our attachment to some sort of ideal (like the philosopher's ideal, truth), some goal of satisfaction, in as complexly psychological a way (neither naturally caused nor reflectively deduced), and then think of that attachment as a condition of life, a condition of any practical sense in a life. The event is not really something that just happens to us, nor something we just decide to do; the exclusive categories of "event *or* action" do not help us understand the phenomenon.

In the second place, these beginning images of eros and the heart, which Nietzsche returns to again and again throughout his works, are not novel or revolutionary, as "the old philologist" no doubt realized. He would clearly have recalled that it was Plato who first character- ized philosophy as essentially a kind of love, as erotic, even divinely, insanely erotic. Philosophy may be the condition of any worthwhile life, but philosophers as a type are not to be distinguished by what they know or by any method. They are distinguishable best by their distinct eros, what provokes or inspires their desire, what grips them. (According to the Diotima's teaching in the *Symposium*, philosophy is properly understood as some sort of higher form of sexual desire.) And Nietzsche is no doubt trying to invoke ironically that Platonic resonance by suggesting that traditional or Platonic philosophers, as conceived Platonically, are actually clumsy, amateurish lovers.

Before exploring in what sense they are clumsy, though, we should note that the image *aligns* Nietzsche with Plato in an important sense. Nietzsche does not treat the desire to know, or the emotional and af- fective aspects of interest in knowledge, in a more familiar, modern sense, as provoked negatively, just by the pain of, the insecurity and weakness caused by, ignorance. At least to some extent, like Plato, Nietzsche treats philosophical desire as originally, actively erotic, not merely reactive or passion-driven. There is something that philoso- phers, or lovers of wisdom, want that they want in itself, positively, independently of any attempt to lessen pain or ignorance. In the classi- cal doctrine, the philosophical soul is thus very close to the tyrannical soul, able to subjugate absolutely everything to a master desire. (In the same way, any erotic love that understands itself as the use of another to satisfy a need is no longer erotic *love*.) So by beginning *Beyond Good and Evil* with the image of philosophical lovers, Nietzsche is pointing to a striving that is not satisfied merely in the absence of pain and the establishment of security but one that always anticipates the satisfac- tions of a possibly better life, not the rendering more secure or com- fortable of the one that one happens to be leading.

In the Platonic presentation there are natural objects of human de- sire and a sort of coherence among the kinds of human wantings and satisfactions. Indeed, for Plato, many of the most important manifesta- tions of human desire already reflect this coherence and intimate the proper satisfaction. Most famously (and controversially), the love of a beautiful body, sexual excitement at the sight of another human be- ing, is already supposed to be an instance of the desire for the eternal possession of the idea of the good. (Hence the central and somewhat hidden assumption of Diotima's account: human, corporeal eros, human love, is supposed to be inherently profoundly frustrating and unsatisfying. Its only value lies in provoking some persons beyond it.) In the *Symposium*, Diotima establishes this striking claim by getting Socrates to agree that everyone who loves anything wants the possession of that thing and does so in the belief that the possession will be good. In her famous ascent, she concludes that contemplating beauty itself is really that for the sake of which all other desires truly desire.[28] Philosophers may begin their careers as lovers in the standard sense, but they come to experience the instability and flightiness of human experience, and the good they admire in the beloved is only a relative and an uncertain good. To love the beauty of a beautiful body is to want to possess that beauty, something that cannot be achieved if we remain attached to the swiftly degenerating body in which it appears. What anyone wants in the beloved can better be found in the beauty of all bodies, the beauty of souls, or good laws; finally in beauty itself, assuming he or she has a strong or powerful enough eros.

The plausibility of Diotima's story depends on something that Nietzsche is most concerned to attack: the assumption that no one could find full or real erotic satisfaction in such a body, or that any finite, limited delight in the corporeally beautiful is ultimately unsatisfying. Such a desired object cannot be possessed *over time*, and so *that* frustration provokes a different sort of attachment, to more universal, less corporeal objects. The whole possibility of a continuous ascent in Diotima's famous account requires some explanation of our dissatisfaction at the lower levels, the provocations that inspire the continuous ascent of eros. Once at 204d, she has Socrates say that the love of good things must be a love for their possession, and at 206a, that "love loves the good to be *one's own forever*," or at 207a, that love is really always of immortality, then the ground is laid for the claims of an ascent. Our attempts to understand the world and ourselves are not provoked merely by the pain of ignorance or the need to satisfy wants and passions. The beautiful, for example, draws us to it, out of ourselves, promising a greater good, not a means to avoid the bad or satisfy the necessary. But, under Diotima's assumption, we also see

28. *Symposium*, 211d.

many instances of the beautiful in changing and degenerating bodies (207d and 207e), and so by being excited by such beauty, come to love the beauty of souls, then just laws, and then the form of beauty itself.

This is the assumption that Nietzsche is disagreeing with, what he is calling clumsy and obtrusive. There is no reason to believe, he is implying, that such an original eros would be experienced as dissatisfying if it could not be redeemed by the kind of security and reassurance promised by Diotima. It is in this sense that philosophers look like amateurish or insecure lovers, as if they demand guarantees, rest, a final respite from insecurity, and so eternal possession. (They can seem like young lovers who must constantly demand from each other pledges of eternal love, as opposed to more experienced lovers, who can love passionately, and not cynically, without such delusory hopes about permanence. We move again here closer to Montaigne and the issue of constant self-overcoming, which will be discussed in chapter 6.) For Nietzsche, the so-called ascent described by Diotima is not an ascent but a *diversion* of eros away from what can only be enjoyed with great risk and uncertainty toward what will satisfy souls already so fearful, even contemptuous of time and finitude. Only under a certain evaluation of life itself, essentially a negative or an ascetic one, would they come to experience desire as they do. (All of this, as an instance of Nietzsche's inversion of the usual psychologizing, is why his remarks about the Platonic account are not that it is false or unsupported, but clumsy, amateurish, inexpert, and so on.) Likewise, the erotic anticipation of wholeness or completeness, so crucial to the Platonic account, would be similarly read in such an account as a hope for and so a projection of the end of instability and unavoidable transitoriness of human desire; in the famous phrase of Nietzsche's, as "revenge against time."[29]

29. Now, at this point, several extended qualifications would have to be made in any fuller assessment of the Platonic position and Nietzsche's treatment. For one thing, Nietzsche's account of Socraticism and Platonism is always resistant (to use what seems the appropriate psychological word) to the manifestly aporetic character of Platonic thought, to the insistence throughout the dialogues that the satisfactions spoken of by Diotima are forever impossible, that whatever slight ascents there might be are always followed by descents, but that eros is sustainable anyway. For another, at the end of the ascent passage (at 212a), Diotima claims that whoever beholds beauty itself "breeds *eidola*," images of excellence. As in the *Republic* and

These remarks introduce numerous issues in both Plato and Nietzsche. I mean only to suggest here that Nietzsche takes himself to be inverting Plato and is treating the desire for the eternal possession of the truth as itself an instance or an example of a different sort of original erotic attachment, already expressive of an evaluation and a perspective, not the natural situation of human beings objectively dissatisfied by corporeal eros. If "truth is a woman," then this last, more sophisticated, unclumsy love at least gives us some sort of trope, a figure, with which to pursue the question of how Nietzsche's philosophers will continue to "love their truths" (*BGE*, §43, 40). It will not be on the condition that some sort of security and stability can be achieved, based on the eternal possession of truth.[30] But it will also not be a mere lust for power or domination or a brute exercise of will or even the way an artist loves what he makes. (We can recall, too, the language of paragraph 226 about how we love "our world," that is, in a way that Nietzsche admits is quite fragile and can fail; it is "barbed, perilous, pointed and delicate [*häklich, verfänglich, spitzig, zärtlich*]" [*BGE*, §226, 117, T].) Here the attachment to one's way of going on, one's perspective, is, while not based on truth, always "truthfully" (or without security, "insatiably") lived.

VI.

What would it mean to satisfy the Nietzschean conditions? We know from any other texts by Nietzsche that there is a great danger that they *cannot* be satisfied, or that desire under these conditions of impermanence, frailty, and contingency can, even in some collective or civilizational sense, fail catastrophically. Nietzsche's rather grandiose word for this failure of desire is *nihilism*. Since nihilism amounts to this

---

Phaedrus, the satisfaction of eros is pregnancy and birth, images of renewal, not eternity. She is, of course, here and in other passages, thinking of beautiful speeches, but the image still stands in marked contrast to Nietzsche's insistence on possession and security. Nothing could contrast more with the hope for eternal security than having children, even if noncorporeal and for the sake of immortality.

30. Recall the original distinction between moralists and metaphysicians: "what these moralists intended merely as approximate signposts or even as no more than truths possessing tenancy only for a decade" (*HAH*, 215).

erotic failure (not ignorance or delusion), addressing it properly becomes quite difficult because, as noted, one cannot be convinced that
one ought to have a desire, that desire ought not to fail, and thereby
acquire it or sustain it. (The most one might be able to do is offer
oneself as an example of such an escape, and here we move closer to
Montaigne again as a model for Nietzsche's enterprise.)

As Nietzsche seems to see it, then, the situation he is confronted
with requires something like a bet, or a wager very different from Pascal's but similar in spirit. The terms of the wager are, What would make
possible a self-sustaining and affirmable (finally, when all is said and
done, beautiful) civilizational project, under current historical conditions? What would make some collective self-transcending aspiration
possible over time, a way of life that would not degenerate, undermine
itself, or, in his apocalyptic word, end in nihilism? (He is obviously
quite pessimistic about the potential erotic power of bourgeois ideals,
such as freedom from external constraint, equal opportunity, security,
or prosperity. "Wretched contentment" he calls that.)

Of course, any option has implications and possible permutations
impossible to foresee, and each will lead to unexpected consequences
in radically altered, future circumstances. One's uncertain situation in
the gamble is thus exactly as Nietzsche describes for his "new species
of philosopher," baptized with "a name not free of danger." "These
philosophers of the future might have the right (and perhaps also the
wrong) to be described as *those who attempt*. Ultimately this name is
itself only an attempt, and, if you will, a temptation" (*BGE*, §59, 39).
(This play on *Versuch*, an attempt or perhaps a gamble, and *Versuchung*,
or erotic temptation, seems to me to confirm much of the interpretation above.)

The question Nietzsche is asking is about the way attachments to
ideals, ideals that orient our inquiry, make possible everything else,
are themselves possible. They are not possible as results of reflection
and deliberation, since the mode of reflection already evinces some
ideal or other of reflective adequacy, relevance, and success. Hence his
questions about what is required for us to love our ideals, especially
now. "What might be possible now" depends essentially on what we
take to have happened, on being able to produce a history that will
show us where we are, what could have been different, and what, in
the light of this, might be appealed to now if we are to continue to

live. Coming to understand this, without ressentiment, is summed up in another famous Nietzschean reference to the problem of love: *amor fati*. To understand what he might mean by this situation, we need to understand the purpose of the book, the title of which immediately dispels the darker and resigned tones of *amor fati*—that is, the promise of a *gay science* (*fröhliche Wissenschaft*).

CHAPTER TWO

What Is a Gay Science?

I.

Nietzsche tells us that he wants to be understood as a psychologist, and he gives us ample reason to believe that the French moralists of the sixteenth and seventeenth centuries, especially Montaigne, Pascal, and La Rochefoucauld, are his models in this enterprise. Several implications follow from taking this suggestion seriously, the most important of which is the "Montaigne problem." That is, how one might combine an uncompromising, brutal honesty about human hypocrisy and bad faith—a realization of the very "low" origins of even the highest of aspirations—with an affirmative reconciliation of some sort with such a weak and corrupt human condition, and all this somehow below, deeper than, the level of conscious belief or attitude.[1] That is, how was it that Montaigne successfully fulfilled the task that Nietzsche attributes to him: "to make [himself] at home in the world" (*UM*, 135)? At least we know already that whatever makes possible such a basic

---

1. In Nietzsche's terms: how is something more than a devaluation possible now; how is a genuine revaluation possible?

orientation (an "attunement" or *Stimmung* in Heidegger's sense), it is not and cannot be the result of a successful "demonstration" about why the world ought to matter in some way or other (unless the availability of such a demonstration itself somehow already matters most).

Although in many contemporary circles, such a psychological interpretation would be characterized as too vague or too literary a view of the main issues in Nietzsche, we have seen that such a psychology is supposed to be *primordial,* even a successor of sorts to "first philosophy." This is because of Nietzsche's claim about the primordiality of issues of value and their psychological conditions.

This claim about primordiality also reframes his relation to the French. That is, his elevation of the French moralists to this rank is already to go well beyond them and their point of view, to make much more of them than they made of themselves, and so, somewhat ironically, to ensure his failure in ever reoccupying their position. That they did not appeal to any deeper philosophical foundation to ground what they wanted to say is not the same as pointing out that there was no such deeper foundation and making something of this absence.[2] As we shall discuss in this chapter, the difference between Nietzsche and the *moralistes français* is largely due to the different historical circumstances under which he must raise the problem of "affirmation." We are burdened "now," Nietzsche believes, by what he calls a different and "heavier" "intellectual conscience," and this creates a "tension" between any possible commitments and passions and this sort of self-consciousness.[3]

II.

Nietzsche did not have available (and anyway would certainly not have used) contemporary language about the pragmatics of intentionality to make this point about "primordiality," but that language is useful in

2. Consequently, there is not much to be gained by adopting the method of the few books and articles that treat Nietzsche's relation to the French, simply listing similar claims and speculating on influence throughout Nietzsche's development.

3. Noticing influences is of course, up to a point, helpful. Nietzsche's emphasis on passion here, and the threat posed to it by reflection, no doubt evinces the influence of Stendhal and especially Stendhal's contrast in *De l'amour* between "le naturel" and "la vanité."

stating the claims, especially since the primordiality point is so important.[4] I suggest that we think of his "primordiality problem" this way.

To know what we ought to believe or are entitled to assert or ought to
do, we need to understand the nature of practical commitments to some
governing standard that we have accepted, one governing what ought
to be believed or asserted or done. To assert that something is the case,
I unavoidably undertake a set of many related commitments to those to
whom I make the assertion, commitments about what else I must affirm
to be true and what I must refrain from asserting, given what I claim.
Some philosophers who hold that "meaning is use" see the meaning of
the expression as simply consisting in these related implied commitments and inferred responsibilities. Some see this network of commitments as demonstrating that even the most basic form of intentionality
requires the play of rational commitments. (Just to be conscious of X is
potentially to claim or judge that X, and so to undertake these commitments and so to be prepared to justify them if challenged.)[5] Nietzsche
would not agree with these implications, but the point here is to note
that the primordiality issue in Nietzsche has to do with value, and in
this case this means something like the basic authority of the constraints
and requirements I undertake to accept, impose on myself, and hold to.
To assert, or to pledge to do, or to claim to know, are thus *au fond* kinds
of promises, and such promises are not explicable as merely natural
events. The constraints we undertake are not the avoidance of or imposed by physical impossibilities. They require my futural commitments
and my holding to them, sustaining them (under some understanding
of, and commitment to, why I ought to), in order to be the promises—
the assertions and expressions of intention—that they are. These sorts
of commitments are thus basic or constitutive for the very possibility
of thought, belief, action, all intentionality. And like many, Nietzsche
would like to understand the source of this normative authority, why
and in what sense we are bound as we are or at least as we seem to be.

4. I am aware that the introduction of the terminology of academic philosophy is
a kind of distortion of Nietzsche, but we need some sort of less figurative language;
pious repetitions of his claims will get us nowhere.

5. Immanuel Kant should get the lion's share of the credit for insisting that intentional awareness is not being *in* a certain sort of state but actively, even "spontaneously," construing that something is the case. See Prauss 1971, Pippin 1981, and
Brandom 1994.

As we have seen, even though he accepts the distinctness of such normative matters, he wants his account to involve and be consistent with what we know about nature. Thus, the famous passage from *On the Genealogy of Morals*: "That particular task of breeding an animal with the prerogative to promise includes ... the immense amount of labor involved in what I have called the 'morality of custom,' the actual labor of man on himself during the longest epoch of the human race" (*GM*, II, §2, 36). A great deal of this labor involves brute physical violence and coercion, but commentators (especially Nietzschean "naturalists") often overlook the fact that such violence is always in the service of some ideal and that the labor does not merely happen but is undertaken, something we do to ourselves. Masters, too, have ideals, and a master "morality" is still in some sense a normative matter, a commitment, not the mere natural expression of a biological type.[6] And to be sure, slavish ideals are "really" strategies of revenge and resistance, but that just means the slaves did not accept being slaves, they *revolted*, even if only "ideologically" and out of fear and resentment. Something *mattered* to them.[7] As we shall see in the last chapter, it is an open question whether Nietzsche can reconcile his views on "self-overcoming"—some sort of negative relation to oneself that is not the traditional divided soul—with his criticisms of the "ascetic ideal," a value he sees still at work in many skeptics, atheists, and humanists.

6. None of this should be taken to imply that such master types have "free will" and can simply resolve whether to engage in master conduct or not. That is as false an alternative as the biological destiny view. The locus classicus for that claim is *BGE*, §21, in which Nietzsche proposes not free or unfree wills but strong or weak wills. It is true that Nietzsche mocks the "slavish" notion that the strong can act otherwise than strongly, but that claim must be connected with his unusual account of agency in general. See the discussion in chapter 4.

7. Thus all the famous backhanded compliments to Christianity, as in the *Genealogy*: "Priests make everything more dangerous, not just medicaments and healing arts but pride, revenge, acumen, debauchery, love, lust for power, virtue, sickness;—in any case, with some justification one could add that man first became an interesting animal on the foundation of this essentially dangerous form of human existence, the priest, and that the human soul became deep in the higher sense and turned evil for the first time—and of course, these are the two basic forms of man's superiority, hitherto, over other animals!" (*GM*, I, §6, 18).

We can see more of what interests Nietzsche by noting that the commitments he is interested in are *dual*. The first we might call a thin or surface commitment of the sort involved when one agrees to play a game or participate in a social practice such as voting, and it consists in what obligations one is in fact undertaking from the point of view of any other player or participant.[8] If you undertake to vote, you obligate yourself to vote in the proper precinct, not to vote twice, and so forth, whether you consciously acknowledge that or not; to play chess, not to move the rook diagonally, and so forth. Playing that game is just constituted by those implications and proprieties. You simply wouldn't be playing if you did not observe them.

But there is another feature of your commitment that is rather a "depth" commitment and, in this analogy, can be said to concern your commitment to the game itself, to its significance. This concerns the difference between voting in a bored and mechanical way just because everyone else is doing it, with little stake in the outcome (but observing the rules, your thin commitments), and voting "as if your life depended on it," with a full or deep (or one might even say "existential") commitment to the practice. (Getting married involves undertaking a set of commitments, but knowing what that set is tells us nothing about *how* one will act out that commitment. Professions of love, on the other hand, cannot be such professions if they only involve a legal pledge to fulfill future commitments.)[9]

With these distinctions in place, we can reformulate Nietzsche's problem and move on to *The Gay Science*. Certain events occur, certain practices are instituted and sustained, because human beings come to be committed to certain norms. These constraints and directives do not merely happen to people; the commitments must be undertaken as such, and they can be and often are abandoned.[10] This undertaking can be somewhat legalistic and thin, but in all distinctly human forms

8. You are also not *playing* the game if you have only learned how to mimic the actions of others in ways that go undetected; you have not thereby *undertaken* to play the game.

9. I am relying heavily in this section on the compelling analysis offered by John Haugeland in his essay "Truth and Rule-Following," in Haugeland 2000.

10. They can be abandoned either because one comes to believe they ought to be or, much more likely, because few people any longer have a stake in the sustaining of the practice or enterprise. The commitment "dies out."

of life, we can also detect some basic, full-blooded or deep, "orienting" commitments.[11] It is usually by means of these latter that collective practices can be sustained over time, resist attack on them, and be resilient to some natural degeneration of intensity. Moreover, these depth commitments can be called basic, because in undertaking them, we are not fulfilling some *other* commitment, as if there could be a universal obligation to undertake some depth commitments. That would obviously start an infinite regress. There does, though, appear to be some hierarchical relation between thin and depth commitments. In speaking or acting, we commit ourselves to a variety of obligations that cannot all be fulfilled, and we need some orienting concern, some general sense of what is more or less important to us, if we are to resolve such conflicts. (As we shall see, it is, however, possible to get by with, let us say, a fairly "thin" depth commitment.)[12]

There is, though, no universal or neutral account of what justifies or warrants or even generally explains such depth commitments, although it already appears that such an orientation with regard to what matters or is of significance must be in some way prevolitional and prereflective (unless the basic commitment is *already* to volitional strength or to reflection). The most we can say is that the commitment is a kind of erotic attachment, as mysterious in its way as the appearance and disappearance of an inspiring eros. (*Depth* would then be another word for a passionate *identification* with a commitment.)[13] As we discussed in the previous chapter, Nietzsche's invocation of eros is, like the Platonic Socrates', very broad and not limited at all to sexual desire. It is, however, important to him that such an aspiration be corporal. Something grips us, it is something we cannot help caring about; it would not be love if it were in the service of some instrumental strategy, and it involves far more than simply a felt desire. It involves a wholehearted, passionate commitment to and identification

11. As I note below, there may not be such deep, or what Harry Frankfurt calls "wholehearted," second-order evaluative attitudes toward first-order desires. See his essay "Identification and Wholeheartedness," in Frankfurt 1988 (164, 175–76).

12. Cf. the way Frankfurt, in another essay, "On Caring," discusses why caring should be understood as a "foundational activity" and as a "fundamentally constitutive feature of our lives" (1999, 162, 163).

13. See Frankfurt 1988, 174–76.

with a desired end. Finally, the commitment question and its psychological conditions are basic because any account of what it is to claim knowledge or recommend action presumes some such always already prior commitments. (So that even "being *generally* indifferent" to the priority or importance of desire satisfaction can count as basic in this way, although that picture can be quite odd, as odd as Bartleby's profound indifference in Herman Melville's story.)[14]

It would thus be correct to say that Nietzsche believes that the normative authority of any goal or object or practice is a result of a certain "projection" of value or self-imposition of authority. He is no realist about value. But this would also be a misleading characterization. No one faces a world of neutral objects and possibilities and "decides" with what sort of importance to invest some any more than one faces an array of persons and decides whom to invest with love. The question of the possibility and the nature of this investment of value that is not really an active projection is what I think Nietzsche means by his primordial psychology.[15]

We can also now say that Nietzsche believes, and is attempting to present evidence for, the claim that the depth of the most important shared commitments in the Christian-humanist form of life is "thinning out rapidly," and the urgent question of "what is possible now" must take some account of historical constraints that cannot be willed away but must somehow be acknowledged; must take account of the absence of any hope for a universal account of "what ought to be valued" and of what now threatens or enhances the possibility of any such ground commitment or erotic attachment.

These reformulated Nietzschean claims raise many questions. Why should we believe there are such commitments? Why can't we treat them as always subject to reflective, rational deliberation? Why are they *so* primordial that they cannot be directly addressed? That is, why

14. I am leaving out here a huge issue: the relevant way to account for these normative/psychological issues in becoming a competent speaker of a natural language. That involves a host of complicated issues, and at this point I am only tracking the core issue in Nietzsche's account, which is much more clearly psychological in its focus.

15. This would be a point of difference with Frankfurt, who makes a good deal out of the *making* up one's mind and the "*deciding*" language of identification.

can't we treat such attitudes as beliefs about what ought to be done, held for reasons that I or anyone can challenge? Is Nietzsche saying that no possibly action-guiding commitment *could* be a result of the exercise of deliberative reason, or is he just saying that, in the cases he is interested in, the empirical evidence is such that that is very unlikely? This would presumably mean that while it might be possible to explain an individual's commitment to, for example, moral equality by saying he became convinced that it was true, in the historical case at issue, given the conditions of slavish life and the ultimate content of the belief, such a rational explanation would be implausible.

Nietzsche addresses these issues in a number of different and sometimes very unusual ways. For one thing, he clearly admits that it *is* quite possible to lead a life without much depth commitment to anything, perhaps because the skeptical climate of late modernity has made such commitments seem impossible to sustain. As we shall see in the next chapter, one of the greatest difficulties in Nietzsche's account of such types—whom he calls the "last men," or "pale atheists"—is that their constant irony, reflexive sophistication, skepticism, and atheism would seem to qualify them as Nietzschean heroes. They certainly are not, but it is not at all easy to say just *what* they might have "gotten wrong" from Nietzsche's point of view. And Nietzsche is certainly not merely encouraging them to be *more* passionate in their skepticism or atheism.

Or, there are some who do not feel the call of any "intellectual conscience" with respect to what they find themselves caring a great deal about. In *The Gay Science,* Nietzsche laments the fact that *"to the great majority* it is not contemptible to believe this or that and to live accordingly *without* first becoming aware of the final and most certain reasons pro and con, and without even troubling themselves about such reasons afterwards" (*GS*, §2, 30). As indicated in the quotation, his "response" to this is just to characterize it as "contemptible [*verächtlich*]."

But in general, Nietzsche's response is much like what we have already seen. For example, believing that I should refrain from acting on some possibility that I find in some experiential way compelling until I can assure myself that such an action would be in principle equally available to all, or until I can be assured that it produces the greatest good for the greatest number—to submit myself to this sort of regulation by considerations of others—cannot be shown to be an unavoidable or some always already presupposed commitment.[16] In fact, just as minimally described, such a self-constraint is, from the point of view Nietzsche is establishing, prima facie, bizarre.[17]

III.

The historical aspect of Nietzsche's primordial question needs to be stressed because the main difference between Nietzschean psychology on the one hand and both Greek and French psychology on the other stems from his insistence on the necessity of a historical dimension to any logos of any psyche, his assumption that psychic functioning is always a second nature, a kind of historical result or product. All this is so even though he never abandons the claim of the second *Untimely Meditation* that such historical self-consciousness is also extremely dangerous and can produce if not handled properly an enervating and immobilizing self-consciousness. He argues there that the "historical sense" (the objective knowledge of the contingent factors that shape a form of life) should never reign "without restraint [*ungebändigt*]." That would be, while "just" in itself in some sense, also unjust to life and its demands, especially too "violent" and deflationary for the "mood of pious illusion" necessary for life, especially because "*it is only in love,* only when shaded by the illusion produced by love, that is to say in the unconditional faith in right and perfection, that man is creative" (*UM*, 95). Indeed, even the *prehistory* of mores involves a long process of training, acculturation, or even "breeding." Accordingly, any account of the soul and the soul's possibilities now must be folded into some sort of historical story.

So Nietzsche's books are not, as they could easily have been, called simply *essais, maxims,* or *pensées.* Many of them announce instead an *epochal* historical consciousness: *The Birth of Tragedy* (a book also,

16. I mean something like Kant's "fact of reason" argument, that the claims of reason, the insistent call of the demand for normative justification among subjects, is in some practical sense unavoidable in order to be free actors at all.

17. If he knew of the famous remark widely attributed to Jonathan Swift, he would cite it: "You do not reason a man out of something he was not reasoned into."

perhaps mostly, about the *death* of tragedy); *Daybreak*; *Beyond Good and Evil*; *The Twilight of the Idols* (*Götzen-Dämmerung*). His major work, *Thus Spoke Zarathustra*, announces the advent of the "last man" and seems to hold out hope for an "overman," a new future species apparently. And of course, anyone who has heard anything at all about Nietzsche has no doubt heard that he announced "the death of God" (*GS*, §125, 119–20). So our first task is to understand what Nietzsche means by adding this historical dimension to his notion of psychology.

We are familiar enough with the metaphor that runs through most of these claims. We might now say that in the Western world, psychoanalysis or even talk therapy itself is "dying out," or that any hope for communism has surely died, or that the epic or tragedies or romanticism have all died out, or that ordinary language philosophy or semiotics have all but died out, and so on. (The image turns up in authors such as Giorgio Vasari and Johann Joachim Winckelmann, too; it is not unique to Nietzsche.) But it is not at all clear what we mean when we say this, since we usually do not mean that some decisive refutation or new discovery has emerged, that what was once believed true is now known to be false, like the cases of astrology or alchemy (if this is even the right account of these events). Successful polemics and discoveries and changing "material conditions" may play their parts but not always the decisive roles, especially when the death and birth issues concern values and norms.

IV.

Looking at the primordiality of psychology in terms of the primordiality of orienting, normative, depth commitments and framing the question about our commitments historically, in terms of their life and now immanent death, brings us to a new sort of assessment and prophecy, a more self-conscious and comprehensive treatment of these "life and death" issues, with the 1882 publication of *The Gay Science*. This is the book that suddenly presents all the images and formulations so famously identified with Nietzsche's name, many for the very first time: nihilism (*GS*, §346), "overman" (*GS*, §143), and in paragraph 125, we hear the first famous announcement by the "crazy man [*der tolle Mensch*]" that God has died and that we have killed him. And we learn for the first time of the strange image that appears to embody figuratively Nietzsche's best hope for some sort of reorientation, some recovery or convalescence from the illness caused by such a death and such a failure of desire, a reorientation and an attitude supposedly provoked by the thought experiment about "the eternal return of the same" (*GS*, §341, 194–95).

If we are to understand Nietzsche's claims in this transitional work of 1882[18] about what has now ended or died and what might possibly begin, what is no longer possible, and what is now, uniquely in human time, possible,[19] we must be able to understand his claim for a radical break with all the authoritative normal "sciences" of the day. This is already apparent in that most unusual title. For what sort of science could support the predicate *gay* or *joyous* (*fröhliche Wissenschaft*)?[20]

The title of the book has a number of resonances. There is, first of all, Emerson, whom Nietzsche always talked about as if he were a

---

18. The publication of the book also marks a personal epoch for Nietzsche. Or so he says himself. The back cover of the 1882 edition proclaims that "with this book a series of Friedrich Nietzsche's writings comes to a close, the collective aim of which has been to set up a new picture and ideal of the free spirit." The books he cites as belonging to that period (this tumultuous period from 1876 to 1882) are *Human, All Too Human*; *The Wanderer and His Shadow* (later published as part of *Human, All Too Human*); *Daybreak: Thoughts about the Prejudices of Morality*; and *The Gay Science*. His themes after this period become broader, the conditions relevant to becoming a free spirit more comprehensive, as he begins to write the three books most responsible for his reputation, *Thus Spoke Zarathustra, Beyond Good and Evil*, and *The Genealogy of Morals*.

19. Nietzsche clearly did not think these epochal moments happened very often. The most obvious forerunner in this respect was Socrates. And there is little doubt that Nietzsche thought he could be the Socrates for his own Alexandrine age, the legislator of new value. Unlike Socrates, Nietzsche took himself to be aware that this could not happen as a result of rational reflection but was essentially a rhetorical achievement and in that sense an aesthetic as well as a political task.

20. I am discussing here what I have also discussed in a more extensive way in Pippin 1999b and Pippin 2000b. The controversial claim at the core of this discussion is that the melancholy of the "madman" who announces "the death of God" in *GS* is treated by Nietzsche as a symptom for which we need the right diagnosis, not as a fate that we are all (including Nietzsche himself) condemned to bear. Appreciating this point and all its implications is the beginning of any successful attempt to understand in what sense a *Wissenschaft* can be *fröhlich*. I summarize that "death of God" interpretation in chapter 3.

seventeenth-century Frenchman. A line from Emerson's essay "History" was used as an epigraph to the first edition of *The Gay Science*, and it raises again what I have called the Montaigne problem: "To the poet, to the philosopher, to the saint, all things are friendly and sacred, all events profitable, all days holy, all men divine."[21] While it is not possible that Nietzsche knew that Emerson had in his journals also called himself a "Professor of the Joyous Science," Emerson did use the same expression in a lecture in 1842, and Nietzsche could have known that.[22]

Another likely source is Thomas Carlyle, who in an 1849 article explicitly contrasted a "gay science" with the "dismal sciences," by which he meant a science that "finds the secret of this universe in 'supply and demand,' and reduces the duty of human governors to that of letting men alone," and so "a dreary, desolate and, indeed, quite abject and distressing" science; "what we might call, by way of eminence, the dismal science."[23]

When such sciences are called "dismal" in this way, the point is not usually to claim that the results of such an investigation make us gloomy or depressed. The point is broader: that such an assessment of human conduct and of value itself already reflects a somewhat low-minded orientation, even a skeptical reduction of noneconomic value to market or exchange value. Likewise, a gay or joyous science is not one the results of which are supposed to make us feel better, happier, and it cannot possibly be a matter just of a more cheerful focus, as if a Nietzschean "look on the bright side of things" were being proposed. Apparently, a different sort of claim to knowledge itself, perhaps even a claim on our attention so different that it won't have even a family resemblance to traditional claims to knowledge, is announced. The problem Nietzsche wants to pose, and so the task for these new scientists—how to *remain* "brave, proud, and magnanimous animals" even in the face of what they discover about motivation and meaning—is what I have called his Montaigne aspirations: to "*know* how to control their own pleasure and pain" (*GM*, I, §1, 12). How does

21. Emerson 1970, 8.
22. Emerson 1972, 367ff. See also Kaufmann 1974, 7-10.
23. Carlyle 1849, 530-31.

one *do* that? What sort of knowledge is that?[24] How do we free ourselves from the grip of a picture of reflection and "doing justice" that
seems enervating in its results?

This is all connected to the clearest historical resonance of the title
of *The Gay Science* rather than to a new social science or new metaphysics, and it again recalls a French "psychological" influence, this time
more archaic: the recollection of *la gaya scienza* and so of twelfth-
century Provençal lyric poetry, the earliest poetry extant in a modern European language, and of the troubadours' art of the fourteenth
century (*Leys d'amors*). Given this reference, what, then, does *such* a
free spirit know in mastering *la gaya scienza*? Perhaps, as Nietzsche
explains, something like what one would have to know to write such
lyrics, or "love as passion (our European specialty)" (echoes here very
clearly from Stendhal), "invented in the knightly poetry of Provence,
by those magnificent, inventive human beings of the 'gai saber.' Europe is indebted to these men for so many things, almost for itself"
(*BGE*, §260, 156). The gay science is, then, a knowledge of erotics; not
so much a knowledge of what love is as how to love and so live well,
and this not technically or strategically but in some way that "does
justice" to the requirements of love and life.

But whatever the original troubadours knew, and so whatever
Nietzsche is trying to rediscover, it comes now with what he calls intellectual and moral "tension," the burden of our "intellectual conscience" or intensely critical self-consciousness, a burden fully and
often acknowledged by Nietzsche. And yet when we look for what
would satisfy this condition, what would give us what Nietzsche
says in *Daybreak* is utterly lacking in our education, "those brave and

24. There are mostly indirect, brief allusions to the issue that the book's title
announces. A typical paragraph is *GS*, §327, where the assumption of an inherent
seriousness in all knowledge (what is later and often figuratively discussed as "the
spirit of gravity") is a "prejudice." Not much is said about what overcoming such a
prejudice would amount to, and the issue is complicated by Nietzsche's use of the
same image when he introduces the Eternal Return notion as, possibly, "the greatest
weight" (*GS*, §341, 194). Its *not* being so experienced is what turns out to be most important in the thought experiment. There is a very suggestive discussion of this and
other similar issues in an article by Marco Brusotti (1997b). His book on the topic
(1997a) is also invaluable.

rigorous attempts to *live* in this or that morality" (*D*, 116, T), we find yet again a cascade of endless, elusive, and highly figurative formulations.

Such a condition for transvaluation suggests a complicated combination of what he calls a lightheartedness or cheerfulness (*Heiterkeit*; *GS*, §343) combined—somehow—with a certain sort of "heaviness" or gravitas (*GS*, §341). Such paradoxical formulations start early in Nietzsche's writing and continue late. What is needed was first thought of as a "tragic pessimism" that would also be an "aesthetic justification of existence," a pessimism but of strength; or a "musical Socrates"; or the ability to "dream" without first having to "sleep" (*GS*, §59, 70). The later preface to *The Gay Science* announces Zarathustra (itself an "awesomely aweless" book) in such a typically dual way: "*incipit tragoedia*," but then "Beware! Something utterly wicked and mischievous is announced here: *incipit parodia*, no doubt" (*GS*, preface, 4).[25]

In many of these images, the same theme is announced, the same "tension" manifested. As Nietzsche would recognize from his reading of Plato (especially *The Republic*), there remains a deep tension between all forms of eros and its satisfactions—often private, incommensurable with others', always only one's own—and justice, the older word for an intellectual conscience, wanting what is fit or mete or fair to want, not what one simply happens to desire passionately. How to measure and assess this counterclaim of "intellectual conscience," in the right way, and how to effect its realization, is what Nietzsche meant by "know[ing] how to control [one's] own pleasure and pain" (*GM*, 1, §1, 11) and poses again the larger question of how to "address" possible commitments that cannot be addressed. "Dreaming" without having to "sleep," loving an ideal without having simply to ignore the demands of reflective adequacy, the possible claims of other ideals, is his figurative statement of the problem. The "tension" formulations certainly indicate that the growth of our intellectual conscience means that our deepest (or "depth") commitments are not immune to the claims of reflection and justification, as if one could be simply strong enough to legislate in defiance of the claims of reflection. (Again, satisfying these claims of conscience is not treated as transcendentally necessary or anything like that. They have simply taken root; we would *now* be ashamed to go

---

25. Cf. Brusotti 1997b on the tension or oscillation (the "*Pendelbewegung*") between *Redlichkeit* ("forthrightness") and *Kunst* ("art") in Nietzsche (Brusotti 1997b, 219).

on without them.)²⁶ Indeed, without that tension, there can finally be no dissatisfaction and therefore no "self-overcoming"; only the easily satisfied "last men" "who have invented happiness" and "who blink."²⁷

There are other such formulations. In *The Birth of Tragedy*, the nature of Aeschylus's Prometheus is "at the same time Apollonian and Dionysian," and that "can be expressed in a conceptual formula" that recalls the theme just introduced: "*All that exists is just and unjust and is equally justified in both*" (*BT*, 51). The promise, in the history essay of the *Untimely Meditations*, to be able to employ history "for life," is also stated explicitly and carefully in the language of justice, as it must be lest this appeal to "history only for the sake of life" turns out to be a call merely for the ideological use of history, even for wishful thinking.²⁸

26. This set of issues is similar to what Bernard Williams discussed in his 1985 book as the relation between reflection (intellectual conscience here) and ethical knowledge (robust commitments here, knowing what is most important) and as the danger that reflection can "destroy" such knowledge. He argues, like Nietzsche, that this is based on several false premises, especially that ethical knowledge is of the propositional sort that could be destroyed by reflection. The contrasting picture he paints of a kind of ethical "confidence" is quite in the spirit of Nietzsche on the health proposed by a gay science (as the mention of Nietzsche on p. 171 indicates). See Bernard Williams 1985, 148, 168–71.

27. Again, the interpretive direction is suggested by an image, this time a Homeric one, a "bow" that must have as much "tension" as possible in order to shoot well, achieve the "target." (We can be said to have "lost" this tension in the late modern age. The image will reappear in chapter 3.) See also my discussion in Pippin 2000a. Nietzsche's appeal to this image means that what would traditionally be categorized as his "political philosophy" starts with a premise that concerns the prepolitical conditions of politics, where politics is understood either as the attempt to determine a legitimate use of publicly controlled coercive force or as a common deliberative attempt to determine the common good. That is, this prepolitical, "psychological" condition cannot be addressed, at least not directly and immediately, by "political" action; it is its presupposition. (Addressing them at all seems to require the highly problematic, dangerous images of "breeding" that we discussed before.) This is a problem of "political psychology" that is as old as Plato's *Republic* but that has been eclipsed by the intense focus that modern political thought devotes to the question of rational legitimacy. I discuss the status of political psychology further in a forthcoming book.

28. Cf. Nietzsche's reminder in *Twilight of the Idols*: "A yearning for strong faith is *not* a proof of a strong faith, but rather its opposite" (*TI*, 198). In *GS*, §324, 181, Nietzsche mentions the most sweeping category in all his accounts of this "tension" problem and announces that what is distinct about his position is that "life" will now serve for him as a "means of knowledge," and this is what will make possible a "gay"

In particular, in an earlier passage from *Daybreak*, Nietzsche had noted that "our passion," "the drive to knowledge," "has become too strong for us to be able to want happiness without knowledge or the happiness of a strong, firmly rooted delusion; even to imagine such a state of things is painful to us! Restless discovering and divining has such an attraction for us and has grown as indispensable to us as is to the lover his unrequited love, which he would at no price relinquish for a state of indifference—perhaps, indeed, we too are *unrequited* lovers!" (*D*, 184). There is no better image of philosophical eros than such an "unrequited love," since it more or less explicitly dominates philosophy's self-image from Socrates on, rendering it useless and even comical in the eyes of nonphilosophers. Its greatest modern proponent was Kant, who claimed not only that human beings are fated to ask questions that they cannot answer but that even the finality of the results of *The Critique of Pure Reason* in setting the limits of knowledge would not put an end to such longing. Indeed, even the resolutely prosaic Kant was inspired to use a variation of the image: "We shall always return to metaphysics as to a beloved one with whom we have had a quarrel."[29] This in effect defines Nietzsche's answer to the question of the philosophical type: it is someone who can sustain an entire lifetime of unrequited love, something that, Nietzsche knew better than anyone, makes the philosophical life a natural subject for comedy.

V.

In *The Gay Science*, Nietzsche finds a way of posing his basic question that allows him to do more than repeat what looks like an interminable aporia. The goal of doing some justice to "love's illusions" (and so an injustice) as well as to our intellectual conscience or to justice is again suggested, but again elliptically and elusively. What is needed now, he says several times, is not some ability to believe whatever will

---

life. This must be coupled with *GS*, §123, 118, where knowledge itself will no longer be a "mere means," not a means to salvation or power or virtue but itself a great "passion [*Leidenschaft*]." Cf. Brusotti's 1997b discussion again.

29. I. Kant, *Critique of Pure Reason*, trans. Paul Guyer and Alan Wood (Cambridge: Cambridge University Press, 1999), A850/B878.

make us strong, or any such fantasy, but a way to "incorporate" or "embody" knowledge (*das Wissen sich einzuverleiben*) and to make it "instinctive" (*GS*, §11, 37). Or we (and I think he means here "we moderns," we heirs of the Socratic enlightenment) have gambled on finding the answer to a difficult question: "To what extent can truth stand to be incorporated [*Einverleibung*]?—that is the question; that is the experiment" (*GS*, §110, 112).[30]

So, following out our "What makes the 'life' of values possible?" question has led us, by attention to the question of what such a "knowledge" would be, or how a science could be joyous, even if also "in bounds" and "just," to an even more unusual question: "To what extent can truth stand to be incorporated?" (*GS*, §110, 112). That is, we know that we are dealing with something more than being persuaded by a convincing argument, more than some acknowledgment that a commitment to act would be reasonable. And we know also that being incapable of such incorporation is a frequent characterization of what we now cannot do with what we take to be true. The reason for this incapacity has to do somehow with a failure of desire and so with Nietzschean claims about contemporary conditions for and the current nature of human desire. Here is a typical (because typically metaphorical) general statement of the theme from the second of the *Untimely Meditations*: "In the end, modern man drags around with him a huge quantity of indigestible stones of knowledge, which then, as in the fairy tale, can sometimes be heard rumbling about inside him. And in this rumbling there is betrayed the most characteristic quality of modern man: the remarkable antithesis between an interior which fails to correspond to any exterior and an exterior which fails to correspond to any interior—an antithesis unknown to people of earlier times" (*UM*, 78).

This all is said to mean that "we moderns" do not have a culture; our culture is not a living thing, it is just the ingestion without digestion of our own past. We are "walking encyclopedias," not participants in a cultural enterprise; the "whole of modern culture" looks like a book titled "Handbook of subjective culture for outward barbarians" (*UM*, 79).

---

30. Cf. Pascal's version of how to achieve such incorporation, in Pascal 1963, §816, §821. On custom and habit, see §81.

This notion of incorporation, of some normative attitude's becoming wholly incorporated, part of us, here evoked by images of digestion, is not a question or an experiment wholly foreign to us. We all have heard someone say, "Yes, I knew that; but I guess I really didn't *know* it." And the problem of judgment lies quite close to this issue, too, as in knowing the difference between homicide and manslaughter (or knowing anything "in theory" or by definition) but not really knowing it in the sense of knowing how to apply the distinction successfully to difficult cases. (Pascal's famous distinction between "l'espirit géometrique" and "l'espirit de finesse" is also relevant.) The distinction between know-how knowledge and knowing-that also seems relevant; propositional knowledge about what to do, such as how to shoot a basketball, only counts as knowledge if embodied, when a part of genuine and largely unreflective know-how. And there is the familiar psychoanalytic case in which the analyst cannot simply tell an analysand the meaning of his neurotic symptoms. Even though the propositions would be true and would be correctly (literally) understood, they would not "really" be understood. A long therapeutic process must have gone on, especially a process of transference and countertransference, before that sort of analytic truth can be fully known, or "digested." Something of all of these uses is being invoked by Nietzsche, especially the last sort of case, but it is difficult to sort out what he is claiming.

VI.

As we have also seen, the conditions under which this could happen are quite complex. Such a revolutionary experiment cannot be arbitrary or wishful thinking, an appeal merely to imagination; "justice" must be done to what has developed as our "intellectual conscience." And that means that the sort of contempt that Nietzsche wants to inspire in us about our present state must account for that state properly, must presume an adequate genealogy, rest on a credible account of psychological meaning. However, as we have also seen, there is no particular reason to think that such an account of real psychological meaning is of any use "from the perspective of life." Such a truth (say, about the slavish origins of Christian and later liberal-democratic value) cannot without further ado be "incorporated," made "instinctual," amount to a *new* sort of depth commitment, as that notion was laid out earlier in this chapter. Sometimes Nietzsche seems to think we will be able to take a kind of pride, retrieve a kind of dignity, from what amounts to our courage, our willingness to face the groundlessness of these commitments in ways no other age has. Again, the early Heidegger is relevant here, since for him, too, death serves as this new god, its utter nothingness at least the occasion of resoluteness and authenticity, and so a kind of nobility.[31] And again there is a similar difficulty. It is hard to see that any course of action or new project is suggested by such a pride. Such a satisfaction in our honesty on its own inspires no course of action or resistance or civilizational project. As Nietzsche puts it in *The Gay Science,* the question remains "whether science is able to *furnish* goals of action after having proved that it can take such goals away and annihilate them" (*GS*, §7, 35).[32] If that truth is *all* that we now stand by, it reduces us to the perspective of that "animal" Nietzsche often mentions when he wants to remind us of how low-minded and practically dangerous such a view, and even his own genealogies, can be: frogs.

What we need of course is *la gaya scienza,* and so far we seem condemned to perpetual introductory circles, careful about what it is not, wary of hastily defining it. But we have come far enough to know what it might mean; that it is a kind of poetry, a love poetry meant to call to mind an extremely idealized love and engaged in not for purely aesthetic reasons but for the sake of some conversion, or seduction, and the attachments and commitments it inspires are a "condition of life." Not surprisingly, there are suggestions, or rather hints, about Nietzsche's response to these concerns, but again, they are implied by a dense and dramatically erotic image. In more traditional philosophical terms, Nietzsche often suggests that we start going wrong when we think of ourselves as having exposed such true groundlessness "underneath" the deceptive appearances, that *this* is what the claim of intellectual conscience has fated for us. And Nietzsche clearly wants to discard as misleading that simple distinction between appearance and

31. See the valuable discussion by Heinrich Meier, "Der Tod als Gott: Eine Anmerkung zu Martin Heidegger [Death as God: A Remark on Martin Heidegger]," in Meier 2003.

32. This is of course the question that Max Weber answers so firmly in the negative in his "Science as Vocation."

reality. He is well known for claiming, in his own miniversion of the self-education of the human spirit in *The Twilight of the Idols*, that "the true world is gone; which world is left? The illusory one perhaps? . . . But no! *we got rid of the illusory world along with the true one!*" (*TI*, 171).

Such a theme introduces far too many issues to allow an adequate treatment here. But since this issue comes up so frequently in *The Gay Science* and is so essential in everything discussed thus far, a brief final discussion of it might at least indicate the direction Nietzsche is suggesting if not a detailed road map showing how to get there.

The image that sums all this up is mentioned at the end of the second-edition preface of *The Gay Science*:

> And as for our future, one will hardly find us again on the paths of those Egyptian youths who make temples unsafe at night, embrace statues, and want by all means to unveil, uncover, and put into a bright light whatever is kept concealed for good reasons. No, we have grown sick of this bad taste, this will to truth, to "truth at any price," this youthful madness in the love of truth: we are too experienced, too serious, too jovial, too burned, too deep for that. . . . We no longer believe that truth remains truth when one pulls off the veil: we have lived too much to believe this. Today we consider it a matter of decency not to wish to see everything naked, to be present everywhere, to understand and "know" everything. (*GS*, preface, 8)

He then anticipates the beginning image of *Beyond Good and Evil*, but now more graphically. "Perhaps truth is a woman who has grounds for not showing her grounds. Perhaps her name is—to speak Greek—Baubo" (ibid.). Baubo is a renowned, clowning, ribald goddess of female sexuality, famous for having made Demeter laugh when that goddess was withholding fertility from the world.[33] She is often portrayed simply as the lower half of the female body, a face on a pregnant belly, a large hat covering the top, and as the bearer of the suggestion that the well-being of the world depends on the satisfaction of female sexuality, something itself lighthearted and joyous. (She

---

33. Nietzsche concludes the "Epilog" to *Nietzsche Contra Wagner* with the same sort of reference to Baubo and uses virtually the same words as the *GS* passage. See *NW*, 282.

is occasionally presented as the personification of female genitalia,[34] and this also jokingly. In fact, a good pictorial summary of her image might be René Magritte's *Le Viol*.)[35] That is, she is another avatar of *Heiterkeit* and a *fröhliche Wissenschaft* and suggests a faith in the "eternal return" of life, an affirmation even in the face of the tragic loss of Persephone.[36] It is also another suggestion that the self-image philosophers have of themselves as courageously trying to see what lies hidden is better understood as an obscene attempt to look up a woman's dress. It is more inappropriate and grotesque than impossible (in Kant's sense of impossible, say), as misguided and crude as trying to find what lies "behind" our basic commitments. (In other words, the way Nietzsche himself is often read, as if a brute desire for power motivates religion, philosophy, poetry, etc.) And one should note immediately, in the grave-robber image, Nietzsche is not denying that there *are* hidden treasures, as well as preserved corpses, of course, inside the pyramids. He appears to be objecting to some kind of abstract separation between inside and outside, denying that either element of the image can be understood without the other, denying that one should be reduced to the other, denying that what should be claimed about the outside or surface is simply the inside or depth.

This suggests one last echo from the original meaning of *la gaya scienza*. In *The Gay Science* (§59), Nietzsche recalls the simple fact that the poetic language of love cannot survive (without loss of meaning) any radical literalization. It is impossible and quite wrongheaded to understand such figurative or poetical expressions as appearances or distortions plastered onto some sober secular truth. Here especially "the truth" does not remain *truth* when the veils are pulled aside, as if the idealizations and appeals to imagination would "mean the same" when "honestly" expressed as some adaptation in an evolutionary game; or if

---

34. This is particularly stressed in Georges Devereux's valuable book (1983), which, besides being an exhaustive account of the details of Baubo in mythology and a summary of many different interpretations, also contains a good catalog of illustrations. (I am grateful to Klaus Reichert for steering me to Devereux's book.) It may sometimes seem that Nietzsche's many erotic images are fairly abstract, or divorced from genital sexuality, but the Baubo references indicate that he was well aware of the corporeal dimensions of the metaphors and similes.

35. See Walker 1988, 235–36.

36. See the discussion in Kofman 1986 (254–59).

expressed in Oedipal, psychoanalytic terms; or if translated into some naturalistic interest in power or satisfaction.[37] It is possible to say that there is some sort of biological drive behind our efforts at reproduction, for example, and even behind the creation of social rules for that process, but it is not possible to imagine such a language of need and drive *employed in an address to another*, as a practical proposal to another, within what Nietzsche has called the context of "life." And yet all of this does not mean that we require some sort of idealized *distortion* of such a nature in order to be able to bear each other's claims on one another. Here the language of appearance and reality breaks down in a way that Nietzsche clearly signals as a model for what he means by, hopes for, in a *gaya scienza*, where that breakdown is taken to heart. We need, he seems to be suggesting, a philosophical language like this erotic language, not a flowery embellishment of a literal truth but one that has overcome thinking of the matter in those alternatives. This would be the "perspective of life" and would be a language capable of appeasing and amusing Demeter, the language of Baubo.

And this way of putting the point makes it clear that Nietzsche also imagines that the experiment in so addressing one another might easily and contingently fail and fail catastrophically; it may just be the case that a sustainable attachment to life and to one another requires the kind of more standard, prosaic "illusion" (a lie) that we have now also rendered impossible. But like all desire, Nietzsche's is, as he says, "unjust" and does not measure itself by the rationally probable. Hence Nietzsche's unusual rhetoric: at once an attempt to shame and to inspire, all by merely manifesting his own aspiration, by offering an image of a life in which what are now taken to be all the possible reflective means of sustaining desire have been lost but that rejects any idea of a merely apparent life's having been revealed. If so, then the most sweeping expression for what is now needed will turn out to be as difficult as it sounds: to sustain the intellectual conscience constitutive of a *philosophical life*, but now without what had been traditionally understood as *philosophy*, the exposure of the reality behind, hidden beneath, the appearances.

---

37. It is a ironic that a large number of interpretations of Nietzsche, especially the so-called naturalist ones, do precisely what he is here forbidding.

CHAPTER THREE

Modernity as a Psychological Problem

I.

Nietzsche's best-known attempt to break the hold that a philosophical or moral picture might have over us is genealogy. At least, genealogy can be liberating in this way if such a genealogy can show us that practices and norms could have been very much otherwise, that some assumption or norm we take for granted as inevitable and unavoidable in fact has a contingent, quite avoidable origin, and an origin considerably more complicated than any notion of "rational commitments" or "reflective endorsement" or "faith in revelation" or the like would allow.

However, I have been trying to suggest that sometimes Nietzsche speculates figuratively on unappreciated, ignored psychological elements of the "picture" itself. Wittgenstein's famous notion of a picture's having a hold on us is largely metaphorical, but Nietzsche explores the picture *as a picture* or an image and plays with the figurative details of the picture itself as a way of defamiliarizing it, changing the way we imagine it, depriving it of its "aura," we might say. He does this with a picture of the value of truth and with a picture of the ends or values of science. This amounts to a kind of rhetorical argument by analogy, one that pivots on an attempt to help us see the traditional picture in a new way. (This somewhat literary approach is also consistent with the constraints Nietzsche had in effect laid down by his denial that philosophical critique amounted to revealing what really lay hidden under the appearances, the denial that we discussed at the end of the last chapter. In effect, he is not looking for what the "morality picture" hides but, more closely, at what it shows.) Once we do see it in this new way, we can come to understand the dispensability or even the arbitrariness of the traditional picture, and we can begin to appreciate the practical need for looking at things a different way. A new picture might come to get a grip on us. That is, the case for such a need is also made somewhat figuratively, as Nietzsche tries to paint a picture of what has turned into ill health, practical unsustainability, and even the "death" of some form of life. Sometimes this sort of case is made in an almost Hegelian or at least more prosaic way, as if various of our practices simply require commitments that are incompatible with one another, and the rational incompatibility of these commitments best explains the weakening hold of some view of norms.[1] But most of the time, Nietzsche's metaphors and images do most of this unusual work by themselves, giving us a different way of understanding what is happening to us. Imagining truth as a woman and philosophers as clumsy lovers is one such attempt; imagining a science that can be "gay," or a science like the original *gaya scienza*, with truth pictured not just as any woman but as Baubo, is another.

In this chapter and the next, I would like to examine two more such alternative psychological pictures. Both will demonstrate that the complexity of the literary dimensions of Nietzsche's project have been strikingly underestimated, that it is far more difficult to ascribe a position to him than has been appreciated. Ultimately this focus will narrow the discussion down to the one image Nietzsche most wants to

---

1. Nietzsche clearly thinks this about Christianity, where the norm for scrupulous honesty about one's motives eventually must raise similar and ultimately destabilizing, embarrassing questions about the motives behind the Christian commitment itself. And the "must" in that claim about issues that "must be raised" is a claim about a kind of practical necessity. All of which is surprising, given the usual views of Nietzsche. Cf., inter alia, *GM*, III, §27.

free us from—the powerful picture of a subject separable from and in effect "commanding" his or her deeds, a distinct causal force responsible for actions occurring and commitments undertaken, something like the pilot of the ship, or a general in charge of her own little army of body movements and vocalizations. As I noted in the preceding chapter, trying to free ourselves of such an image without introducing another picture just as inappropriate, that of some sort of subjectless play of anonymous forces, will be the crucial test of what Nietzsche is trying to convince us of.[2] The first image that I would like to discuss is in fact a little parable.

II.

Paragraph 125 in Nietzsche's *The Gay Science* is perhaps the most famous passage in all of Nietzsche. In it, Nietzsche introduces a character, *der tolle Mensch* ("the crazy man"), who proclaims that God is dead and that we all collectively have killed him, that all must bear the burden of guilt (for centuries) for this horrible murder. Like other famous images in philosophy, like Plato's cave or Descartes's evil genius or Kant's island of truth surrounded by seas of illusion, the passage has taken on a life of its own quite independent of its place and function in *The Gay Science*, the book that may be Nietzsche's most beautiful and best thought out. It has come to represent and sum up not just the unbelievability of God in the late modern world but the "death" of a Judeo-Christian form of moral life, the end of metaphysics, or the unsuccessful attempt to end metaphysics, or even the end of philosophy itself.

   Yet the passage is also quite mysterious and suggests a number of interpretive problems. As we have seen, the very idea of a death or an end to a form of life (rather than a refutation or an enlightenment) is worth considerable attention in itself, but the literary details of this

---

2. One of the few commentators to appreciate the importance of the literary elements of Nietzsche's style is Sarah Kofman (1972). As will be very clear, I disagree with almost every aspect of her interpretation, but she sees clearly what needs to be accounted for in Nietzsche's texts.

little drama are even more striking.[3] The announcement is made by a
crazy man who carries a lantern although it is broad daylight;[4] says
that he is seeking a God who, he clearly knows, does not now exist;
and after proclaiming that the time for such announcement is not right
and that he will never be understood, promptly begins his prophetic
activity anew and with even more intensity (breaking into churches
and screaming his message at the assembled multitude). He is clearly
crazy, but in what sense is he crazy?[5] There is of course a "romantic"
sense of insanity as the inevitable price of authenticity or integrity, according to which it is the unusual depth or profundity of the insight
itself that drives one crazy, a successor notion to the mythic sense that
God may not be viewed by humans. His absence apparently cannot be
borne either, according to such a romantic view.

But the announcement itself suggests a kind of insanity more directly. On the face of it, the announcement that "God is dead" is, even
metaphorically, opaque. If there had been a *god*, we could not have
killed him. That is, if we could have killed him, he could not have
been a god in anything like the Judeo-Christian sense. If "God" existed
only as a constructed object of belief—a kind of collective "illusion,"
in Freud's famous claim—then exposing this illusion might be unset-
tling and make for much anxiety. Afterward, it might be impossible
to return to the same illusion. But such unease could not be about a
"death," or, especially, *guilt* at having "caused" it, even if one reads the
claim metaphorically (as in "*We* destroyed the old illusion that there
was a god"). If that were the meaning intended, the only guilt relevant
would be guilt at having allowed ourselves to have been so deceived

3. Nietzsche is obviously suggesting that this death is not rightly understood as
the inability to believe a proposition. (And, if that is so, if the phenomenon is more
like what the religious call "losing faith," then the original, being religious, is not
originally and solely a matter of belief.)

4. This is an obvious reference to Diogenes, who did the same thing, but instead
of searching for *un homme honnête* (as Nietzsche is, I have suggested, following Pascal), he searches for a God who, he knows, no longer exists.

5. I discuss these aspects of the passage in much more detail in chapter 6 of the
second edition of *Modernism as a Philosophical Problem* (Pippin 1999a, 144–59). The
focus there is on the unusually apposite relevance of Sigmund Freud's differentia-
tion between "mourning" and "melancholy" to the psychological problem Nietzsche
wants to diagnose.

and could not be guilt at ending the delusion.[6] Indeed, it is a striking fact that Nietzsche himself provides, in his own voice, not the voice of a persona, a much simpler gloss on the claim and one far different in tone. He explains in *The Gay Science* that "the greatest recent event— that 'God is dead'" should simply be taken to mean "that the belief in the Christian God has become unworthy of belief" (*GS*, §343, 199, T).

So the oddness of the language in paragraph 125 of *The Gay Science* itself, and Nietzsche's own very different gloss (especially since the theme of that later passage in book 5 is "cheerfulness," not guilt),[7] directs our attention to the contrasting uncheerful, indeed morbid tone of the first passage, the famous locus classicus often cited as Nietzsche's own "belief" that "God is dead." (Nietzsche's cheerfulness, *Heiterkeit*, is the important issue here because the most important question at stake for him since the encounter with the French moralists in the late 1870s is the possibility of a *"gay science"* and so not nihilism and guilt. This passage is the turning point in avoiding La Rochefoucauld's cynicism and Pascal's despair and approaching what he called, in praising Montaigne, "a coming to rest within oneself, a peaceful being for oneself and breathing out,"[8] what Montaigne himself had described as "C'est une absolute perfection, et comme divine, de sçavoir jouyr loiallement de son ester.")[9] It would seem that Nietzsche is trying most of

---

6. We could be said to feel responsibility, perhaps guilt, if we helped render the belief in God less credible, and so made much more painful the lives of millions who appear to need this illusion very badly, but, aside from a very small number of people, the announcement can hardly be said to have had that effect (as the end of the parable makes clear), and the passage suggests guilt about having "murdered God," with bloody knives even, not guilt at the effects of such a "murder."

7. Cf. Nietzsche's praise of Montaigne's cheerfulness, *"Heiterkeit,"* and his contrast between two forms of *Heiterkeit* in the third of the *Untimely Meditations*. The language he uses to describe what he thinks Montaigne has avoided sounds as if addressed directly at the "crazy man's" histrionics. "There are two very different kinds of cheerfulness. The true thinker always cheers and refreshes, whether he is being serious or humorous, expressing his human insight or his divine forbearance; without peevish gesturing, trembling hands, tearfilled eyes, but with certainty and simplicity, courage and strength, perhaps a little harshly and valiantly but in any case as a victor" (*UM*, 135).

8. This is from "Richard Wagner in Bayreuth," or the fourth essay of the *Untimely Meditations* (207). The translation has been amended; the German reads: "ein In-sich-zur-Ruhe-kommen, ein friedliches Für-sich-sein und Ausathmen" (*KSA*, vol. 1, 444).

9. Montaigne 1962 (III, xiii).

all to draw critical attention to, rather than express or identify with, the "melancholic" tone, both of the announcement and perhaps of the coming modernist culture of melancholy, the tone appropriate to the belief that a kind of death has occurred, that we were responsible, and that this death results only in some unbearable, frightening absence. So the most extraordinary feature of the history of the reception of the passage is that what seems clearly to be a kind of symptom of a modern pathology, for which Nietzsche wants a diagnosis and some sort of cure, is often taken *as* the diagnosis of the modern "orientation" or mood itself. The picture he wants to free us from is the most familiar picture we have of Nietzsche![10]

The most significant feature of the passage concerns what Nietzsche appears to think the appropriate response to this announcement should be. In setting the context for the announcement, especially in describing the audience to whom it is made, Nietzsche goes out of his way to suggest that what we normally regard as "atheism" is far too simplistic a description of what it would be truly to "incorporate" this truth. The opening passage describes as the madman's audience a group of people who "did not believe in God" and, when they hear the madman proclaim that he seeks God, jeer sarcastically and joke, "Has he been lost, then?" "Did he lose his way like a child?" "Is he hiding?" "Is he afraid of us?" "Has he gone to sea?" But if the madman is mad, these jeering atheists are clearly portrayed, as they are elsewhere in

10. I have tried to show (Pippin 1999a) that Nietzsche is here anticipating Freud's famous distinction between mourning and melancholy in reaction to a loss or trauma and so is suggesting that the madman's madness is this kind of melancholic obsession with what has been lost, complete with its narcissistic assumption of grandiose responsibility, lurid details of murder and blood and guilt, and repetitive compulsion. What is most revealing is what Freud says about melancholy: "Melancholy is psychically designated by a deeply painful disturbance, by a suspending of interests in the external world, *by a loss of the capacity to love*, by a restriction in activity and an emphasis on a feeling which expresses itself in self condemnations and complaints against oneself and which escalates to a deluded expectation of punishment" (Freud 1963, 165; my emphasis). (The fact that the madman's reaction is pathologically melancholic does not mean that Nietzsche is trying to "ironicize" the entire issue, as if the madman were simply mistaken or neurotic. He certainly does mean to suggest that we have only just begun to appreciate how much will change once the "event" is properly digested. See, for example, *TI*, "Skirmishes of an Untimely Man [*Steifzüge eines Unzeitgemässen*]," §5.)

Nietzsche, as thoughtless, smug, self-satisfied boors. In other passages, Nietzsche's Homeric epithet for such atheists is *"pale* atheists," suggesting this lack of vitality or even sickness.[11] So we need to understand why, if the death of God signals a general end to the possibility of transcendence, religion, morally significant truth, and so forth, the successor culture would *not* simply have to be a culture of such pale (joking, ironic) atheists, people for whom nothing much is important beyond their own immediate happiness and their security in achieving future happiness.[12] If Nietzsche wants to suggest that the madman is pathologically wrong to treat the absence of God as a loss, wrong to take on the burden of a self-lacerating guilt, he seems just as dissatisfied with these "village atheist" types who are too easily satisfied with a secular materialism and easy unbelief and so do not understand the erotic aspirations and ideals Nietzsche elsewhere treats as "a condition of life."

Thus the question is, why does Nietzsche treat these self-satisfied atheists this way? *What* are they missing? What does Nietzsche want us to understand by his rejecting both the notion of a now absent God *and* the stance of what appears to be straightforward, enlightenment atheism?[13] In his own terms, this means understanding why a life guided by the "old values" is just as impossible as a life guided by "no values," or with only the weakest of general or depth commitments, and so why a "transvaluation," an *"Umwertung"* of all values is what is now necessary, and what it would be like.

11. See especially *GM*, III, §24, 117. With reference to my thesis in this book, note also: "NB!! Hence one finds less free thinking [*Freisinnigkeit*] among atheists than among the pious and believers when it comes to moral things (e.g. in moral questions Pascal is freer and thinks more freely than Schopenhauer)" (*NF* [1887], *KSA*, vol. 12, 321). And this more lighthearted note on atheists from *Ecce Homo*, in reference to Nietzsche's admiration for, even envy of, Stendhal: "He beat me to the best atheist joke, just the sort of thing that I would say: 'God's only excuse is that he doesn't exist'" (*EH*, 91).

12. I am grateful to Irad Kimhi for several conversations about this problem in particular.

13. It is certainly true that these atheists do not yet appreciate that a great deal more of the stability of their moral lives is affected by the "death of God." They do not appreciate that their whole picture of human psychology, human sociality, and virtually all nonreligious value is now threatened, that belief in God cannot be so isolated and simply given up. But in the terms used below, that is still too "intellectualist" a picture, as if there is something more they must come to understand. That is at best a half-truth; whatever they lack, it cannot be provided by enlightenment.

III.

Nietzsche's most comprehensive and best-known term for the historical and psychological situation that in the present age requires this
"transvaluation of values" after "the death of God" is *nihilism*, and that
larger discussion sets out a bigger stage on which Nietzsche can present what he thinks will avoid the pathological response of the madman and the insipid and self-satisfied secularism of the last men and
pale atheists.

The surface meaning of these claims about the *nihil*, about the absence that necessitates a transvaluation, has suggested many different
kinds of provocations and so raises questions about how Nietzsche
wants us to understand the conditions possible now (without *God*,
in all senses of the term) for the success of that activity he treats as
identical to a distinctly human living: esteeming, *schätzen*, valuing.
("Human," Zarathustra says, means "the esteemer" [*TSZ*, 43].)[14] The
possibility of sustaining a commitment to any such value in the current historical condition, a condition of cultural or spiritual death, is
the "psychological" question we have been following throughout.

On the one hand, the problem of nihilism can look like a problem
of knowledge, or at least reasonable belief. What had once seemed
known, or worthy of belief, now seems a "lie," "unworthy of belief."
Such cognitivist terms suggest an anthropologist watching the disen-
chanting enlightenment of a primitive tribe, and so the notion appeals
to such double-edged enlightenment as the best explanation for how
we have come to be the first civilization that must live self-consciously
without any confidence that we know what civilized life is for.

On the other hand, especially when Nietzsche is trying to draw a
distinction between what he calls a passive and an active nihilism,
what we have come to claim to know or to believe, while important,
is not the chief issue. "Active" nihilism is interpreted as a "sign of in-
creased *power* of spirit"; "passive" nihilism as "decline and recession of
the *power* of spirit."[15] These passages take a familiar skeptical attitude

14. The point is made again in *GM*, II, §8, 49, where man is called "the calculating
animal as such [*das abschätzende Tier an sich*]."

15. Cf. the passage from *Twilight of the Idols*: "Whoever doesn't know how to put
his will into things at least puts *meaning* into them: that means, he has faith that a

about the practical implications of any putative intellectual enlightenment. Claims about value do not, for Nietzsche, report the discovery of moral facts but express, enact, encourage, and partially realize a commitment. Giving a genealogy of such commitments can never be completed by an inventory and evaluation of theoretical beliefs; something else must always be added. It has seemed to many modern philosophers that such an addition must be a kind of *subjective* reaction—an outpouring of sympathy, a recoil in pain, the stirring of a passion—and therewith a "projection of a value" as a way of embracing or rejecting some situation. This is not Nietzsche's position (although he certainly often says things that sound like this), but for now we need only note that while we can base reasons to act or to undertake commitments on such beliefs (as has often come to be the case, given our "intellectual conscience"),[16] the strength or weakness of the theoretical claim about "what there is" is not itself an independent factor in such commitments, in such acts of valuing. Acting is *negating* what there is and so presumes some sort of experience in which such an absence or a barrier or a limitation or a simple fact becomes unacceptable, not merely noted; it is something that must be overcome. Acting in the light of this unacceptability is "acting for a value," and what we are in effect looking for is the source and meaning of such unacceptability, given the death of God, the absence of any notion of a natural completion or telos, natural law, common human nature, or some objective ideal or divine legislator, and also given the gross simplicity of any attempt to try to will to reinvest the world with some new, life-affirming value.

In summary, then, we have been investigating how Nietzsche understands the psychological conditions of value, the possibility of an action-guiding depth commitment. He treats the current context as hostile to this possibility both because of the death of God and even more because of how that news has been understood. For a number of reasons, previously orienting commitments have lost their

---

will is already there (principle of 'faith')" (*TI*, 158). And compare: "It is a measure of the degree of strength of will to what extent one can do without meaning in things, to what extent one can endure to live in a meaningless world because one organizes a small portion of it oneself" (*NF* [1887], *KSA*, vol. 12, 364).

16. See *GS*, §110, 111, on how our commitments to knowledge and truth came to "take their place as needs among the other needs."

credibility and, more important, their ability to inspire sacrifice and dedication, and the disorientation brought about by this collapse has been intensified by two forms of pathological reaction: a melancholic and ultimately narcissistic theatrical guilt and a self-satisfied pose of supposedly enlightened freethinking. These reactions also rest on misdiagnoses (themselves symptoms of underlying psychological conditions), treating nihilism either as a direct consequence of intellectual enlightenment or as if a result of a courageous decision to "pull out" the value in the world that we had naively "put into it" before.

IV.

What I want to suggest at this point is probably predictable by now: that we treat the phenomenon of nihilism in a way closer to Nietzsche's images and figures and tropes, many of which have been cited often; images of death, decay, illness, the absence of tension, a "sleep" of the spirit (as in his beautiful claim that what is needed now is "an ability to dream without having to sleep"), and perhaps the most intuitive metonymy of failed desire: boredom.[17] These images suggest that the problem of nihilism does not consist in a failure of knowledge or a failure of strength or courage or will but a *failure of desire*, the flickering out of some erotic flame. Noting as we have how often and with what significance Nietzsche refers to life and the "perspective of life" as the issue of an erotic striving, that his question is "what makes possible the origination of such a wanting," what sustains it and the sacrifices it calls for, and so forth, casts a different light on the nature of the "death of God" or nihilism crisis and on what Nietzsche regards as a possible way out of it. It frames all the issues differently, especially since the failure of desire can be baffling, quite mysterious,

---

17. Cf. *HAH*, 390; *BGE*, §228, 118. In *BGE*, §254, the passage in which he praises France as "the seat of the most spiritual and sophisticated culture in Europe today" (*BGE*, §254, 145) ("der Sitz der geistigsten und raffinirtesten Cultur Europa's"), he attributes much of the boring quality of German life to Germans' lack of experience of and their innocence in "voluptate psychologica." Cf. also Heidegger's interesting shift in emphasis, in his lecture course of 1929–30 (*Die Grundbegriffe der Metaphysick. Welt—Endlichkeit—Einsamkeit*), from anxiety to boredom as an ontologically revelatory state (1975ff., 29–30:244, 248).

not something that in some other sense we ever "want" to happen, as mysterious as the issue of how one might address such a failure. (More about this in chapter 6.) And, as we saw, none of the reformulations can appeal to any simple "naturalism." That is, what Nietzsche is talking about is clearly not the mere *presence* of powerful urges or passions or their matter-of-fact absence. We can experience such urges without "committing" ourselves to them; we can even have contempt for our own passions and for ourselves for having them. It is the possibility of a second-order passionate identification with some possible project or goal, some dedication to a hierarchy of what matters, that interests Nietzsche and that raises the questions of how he understands the possibility of the self's "negative" relation to itself and what would, in the historical situation he describes, make possible a way of addressing that "negativity" or self-dissatisfaction.[18]

This image of the passionless, bored bourgeois has by now become a rather banal cliché, in large measure thanks to Nietzsche. There are two elements that are striking (and underappreciated) in Nietzsche's account of this phenomenon: (1) that *so* much is at stake for him in this sort of fate: the unsustainability of "values" and assumptions we would otherwise think are simply indispensable for any coherent life; and (2) the role of various images of eros or striving in his narrative. The erotic images that refer to such a basic commitment repeat, become like motifs in Nietzsche's work. One example of these images states a problem that has clearly emerged from what has been said above and will occupy us for the rest of this chapter and much of the next. In *Thus Spoke Zarathustra*, Zarathustra announces the advent of nihilism as an erotic problem this way: "Beware, the time approaches when human beings will no longer launch the arrow of their longing

18. Stating properly Nietzsche's position on nature and naturalism is quite difficult. He clearly wants to distinguish himself from reductionism and the dismal science of the English genealogists. An example of the difficulty is the following remarks about Montaigne: "Even Montaigne is a naturalist in ethics compared to the ancients, though an endlessly richer and more thoughtful one. We are thoughtless naturalists, and are fully conscious of it [*Auch Montaigne ist den Alten gegenüber ein Naturalist der Ethik, aber ein grenzenlos reicher und denkender. Wir sind gedankenlose Naturalisten und zwar mit allem Wissen*]" (*NF* [1873–74], *KSA*, vol. 7, 741). There is another essay one could wish for from Nietzsche in *Ecce Homo*—"How I Avoided Becoming a 'Gedankenlose Naturalist.'"

beyond the human, and the string of their bow will have forgotten how to whir" (*TSZ*, 9). In the preface to *Beyond Good and Evil*, he notes that our long struggle with and often opposition to and dissatisfaction with our own moral tradition, European Christianity, has created a "magnificent tension [*Spannung*] of spirit in Europe, the likes of which the earth has never known: with such a tension in our bow we can now shoot at the furthest goals" (*BGE*, preface, 4). But, he goes on, the "democratic enlightenment" also sought to "unbend" such a bow, "to insure that spirit should not experience itself so readily a 'need'" (ibid.). This latter formulation coincides with a wonderfully lapidary expression in *The Gay Science*. In discussing "the millions of young Europeans who cannot endure boredom and themselves," he notes that they would even welcome "a yearning to suffer something in order to make their suffering a likely reason for action, for deeds." In sum: "neediness is needed! [*Not ist nötig*]" (*GS*, §56, 64). (One of his most striking formulations of the death of desire occurs in *Ecce Homo* in a telling passage that has received almost no comment, even though it is a wonderful summary of the uniqueness of his position. He notes what is happening to us as "one mistake after another is calmly put on ice; *the ideal is not refuted—it freezes to death*" [*EH*, 116].)[19]

In the context of these images, the possibility of picturing a state of character or social organization as valuable is what it would be for it to inspire a deep commitment to it, somehow to create a longing for such an object, or to find others in whom a possible spark of such longing could be discovered and fanned. Such a possibility is hard to imagine, since no subject, however strong-willed, could simply inject such erotic value "into" the world from a position "outside it" like this. Any such desire can only be found and inspired and sustained *in* a certain sort of world, a world where some intense dissatisfaction can be balanced by an aspiration at home in that very world, a world, in other words, lovable enough to inspire as well as frustrate.[20] Inspiration of this sort can create what Nietzsche has been calling the "tension" in a bow and what I have termed Nietzsche's account of the self's "negative" relation to itself. This tension, that is, amounts

19. Trying to "refute" an ideal is called an "idealism" (a faith in the autonomy of ideals) and is rejected. Ibid.

20. Cf. on this topic the valuable discussion by Lear (1990, 132–55).

to Nietzsche's term for self-consciousness, the possibility of some distance from oneself that makes possible everything from there being possible addressees of Nietzsche's rhetorical appeals to rendering intelligible that one could not *be* who one is, might thus have to become, would want to become, who one is.

However, on the other hand, fidelity to Nietzsche's images seems to make things even more puzzling. For the question of the possibility of such an appeal and response is always treated as a *historical* possibility (or absence of possibility) by Nietzsche, even given the warnings of the second *Untimely Meditation*. This embeddedness of such a subject adds to the difficulty. Consider this summation of the issue (a passage that also renders pretty irrelevant both most of Heidegger's great dissatisfaction with Nietzsche as well as the subjectivist/projection, neo-Humean readings of Nietzsche on value): "The whole attitude of 'man *against* the world,' of man as a 'world-negating' principle, of man as the measure of the value of things, as a judge of the world who finally places existence itself on his scales and finds it too light—the monstrous stupidity of this attitude has finally dawned on us and we are sick of it; we laugh as soon as we encounter the juxtaposition of 'man *and* world,' separated by the sublime presumptuousness of the little word 'and'!" (*GS*, §346, 204). And Nietzsche was very well aware, from early in his writing career, that this unusual diagnosis of the condition of nihilism meant that strategies for addressing it were also going to be unusual, difficult, perhaps impossible. In "Schopenhauer as Educator," he notes a difficulty that suggests a tragic pathos to this position. "It is hard to create in anyone this condition of intrepid self-knowledge because it is impossible to teach love; for it is love alone that can bestow on the soul, not only a clear, discriminating and self-contemptuous view of itself, but also the desire to look beyond itself and to seek with all its might for a higher self as yet still concealed from it" (*UM*, 163). And in *The Gay Science* (§334, 186–87), he had noted that all love has to be *learned*. "Even he who loves himself will have learned it in this way—there is no other way. Love too must be learned." And from *Daybreak*: "All our thinking and poetising, from the highest to the lowest, is characterized, and more than characterized, by the excessive importance attached to the love story: on this account it may be that posterity will judge the whole inheritance of Christian culture to be marked by something petty and loony" (*D*, §76, 77, T).

V.

Passages about eros and about the worldliness of eros have not, of course, been wholly ignored, but, as alluded to above, they are often folded into a general discussion of Nietzsche's views on the body, his supposed naturalism, and what he often refers to as the problem of instincts. And there is no particular reason not to see this emphasis on constant, powerfully motivating, human longing (or the enervating experience of its failure) as an aspect of what Nietzsche talks about elsewhere as instinctual forces (or their absence). (In *this* sense, he would again agree with Montaigne's claim that the human "condition est merveilleusement corporelle" [Montaigne 2002, 673].)

But again, as the emphasis on the presence or absence of "tension" has already revealed, a wholly naturalistic account would be much too hasty here. The very multiplicity and range of the different possible drives appealed to and the fact that Nietzsche's accounts of pre-volitional drives and instincts are often as much historical as organic (tied essentially to a specific historical self-understanding) indicate already that the basic psychological questions for him have remained interpretive, still essentially questions about the weight or significance of the corporeally pressing, however intense; the basic possible response to such embodied interpretations is a matter of *Bildung* or culture, not—or not any longer—the threat of sticks or the promise of carrots.[21]

According to Nietzsche, we are now in a position of tremendous collapse, flux, and uncertainty because of the failure of desire that he calls nihilism, and he clearly thinks there must be some—even if very indirect, unusual—way to *address* that failure. The most important of

---

21. Thus, from *The Gay Science*, "that a violent stimulus is experienced as pleasure or pain is a matter of the *interpreting* intellect which, to be sure, generally works without our being conscious of it" (*GS*, §127, 122). And especially in *Human, All Too Human*: "Because we have for millennia made moral, aesthetic, religious demands on the world ... this world has gradually *become* so marvelously variegated, frightful, meaningful, soulful, it has acquired colour—but we have been the colourists" (*HAH*, 20). See also *D*, §103, 60 (that we must learn to think differently before we can "perhaps very late [*vielleicht sehr spät*]" learn to feel differently), and a very clear statement of the same point at *D*, §35, 57.

the psychological issues he must deal with is what he had called this "tension" in the bow, the way a soul can be said to pull against itself, a tension I suggested was the way Nietzsche understood the phenomenon of self-consciousness itself, the basic reason why a subject could never be said to *be* an object or a thing but can be, even at its most self-affirmative, also always in a negative relation to itself.

As we shall see in the next two chapters, this idea plays an important role in the distinction that he clearly everywhere assumes but does not specifically account for—the difference between a human action and an ordinary event. Nietzsche wants to make this distinction without reintroducing the standard Christian-liberal picture of individual reflective deliberation, endorsement, and causal power. In this context, the question concerns the psychological possibility of something like a reflective stance toward oneself (that "being a subject" is not like "*being* an animal" or "*being* white") and a kind of responsiveness that could account for some new sort of mobilization and direction of psychic energy and commitment. Nietzsche's rhetoric is not at all consistent with the picture of fixed natural types (master or slave types, say) merely expressing their inherited drives, so that the problem would be just finding a way to allow this to happen more robustly, to clear away the many barriers and internal monitors that the clever slavish types have constructed for millennia. This tension, while it is perfectly consistent with a naturalism and presumes no dualism, is hardly a matter of basic drives just *being* in conflict or tension. The self-relation in question is everywhere interpretive and evaluative, involves a self-dissatisfaction, not the pull of some other inclination, and so the question Nietzsche is raising concerns both the possibility of this self-contempt and what it would then mean to address it in some way, why one would address it.

VI.

Nietzsche's account of this tension or self-dissatisfaction is essentially historical. The psyche amounts to a historically achieved and quite variable way of holding ourselves and others to account. For example, in the *Genealogy* he insists that quite a complex and difficult social and historical achievement is necessary before it would even begin to make sense to evaluate ourselves and others with the notions of "intentional," "negligent," "accidental," "accountable," and their opposites (*GM*, II, §4, 43). This capacity for resistance and negating power he calls "the instinct for freedom," which he says is just another way of naming his "will to power" (*GM*, II, §18, 64). We can, he says in that same paragraph, formulate an ideal of beauty and make sacrifices, indeed suffer for it, only because we have first recoiled from the ugly *as ugly* (that is, not simply recoiled from an object).

This historical narrative does, though, make a very minimal assumption about the "nature" out of which such historical development proceeds. As he puts it in the first paragraph of the second essay of *On the Genealogy of Morals*, the problem of breeding an animal capable of promising is a "task [*Aufgabe*]" that nature "has set herself" (*GM*, II, §1, 38). Nature "sets the task" that human beings must complete in historical time because any conceivable human situation is one in which suffering is unavoidable, and Nietzsche claims throughout the last two essays of the *Genealogy* that it is suffering that in effect shocks, provokes human beings into a complex response, not just reactions of avoidance and a policy of prudence. He gathers whatever historical, anthropological, literary, and philological elements he can muster to try to demonstrate that a species-distinct reaction is also provoked; that is, the burden of the question of *the meaning of suffering* is taken on. He assumes that we are so disposed that the deepest suffering we can experience is from a lack of any sense in the suffering. Consciousness itself is often treated by Nietzsche as such a reactive phenomenon, as if human beings do not merely suffer but, given the intensity of their suffering and some sort of disposition to react against it, they can be said also to be jolted into the awareness *that* they are suffering, and this not just as a kind of second-order neutral self-monitoring. Such second-order awareness is originally reactive and negative, seeks to cancel out in some way what injures so meaninglessly. For example, in the case of primitive injuries by others, he tries to show that we can retroactively render the act in some way sensible by requiring recompense from the offender. "What suffering means" is that balance has been upset and can be restored, usually by payment in the suffering of the offender; more precisely and gruesomely, by pleasure in watching the other suffer. His story then develops into the famous account of bad conscience, internalization and sublimation, guilt and debt, the ascetic priest and ascetic ideal.[22]

This is a thought—that human nature is such as to deny itself its natural situation, that human nature just is a disaffection with its own nature—that resonates with many philosophers whom Nietzsche would disown but who form an exclusive club. It is the founding thought of a decisive strand of modern philosophy—Jean-Jacques Rousseau's thought, and thanks to Rousseau, it shows up in Kant's account of our "unsocial sociability [*ungesellige Geselligkeit*]," in Hegel's account of the nonnatural claim of the other for recognition, and in Marx's famous account of the significance of socially organized labor. It shows up for different reasons in Freud's account of the harshness of the repression of natural (essentially Oedipal) desire and so our self-division (the self-division that makes us human, allows it to be said that we lead lives rather than merely exist). The somewhat mythic picture here is straightforward: the natural world is a world without genuine individuality (just mere particularity, in Hegel's language), is formless, brutal, chaotic, and indifferent, and to live a human life is (and essentially is *only*) to *resist* this, to *make* oneself *something* other than this, all because, at least up till now, we have not accepted it and have found a way to provoke such dissatisfaction in others and for posterity. This resistance amounts to achievement of what Nietzsche calls "the sovereign individual" (*GM*, II, §2, 40), in which individuality is understood as always a kind of fragile, unstable, threatened *achievement*, not an original state of being.[23] Nietzsche clearly wants to raise

22. Cf. *GM*, III, §15, 100: "'I suffer: someone or other must be guilty'—and every sick sheep thinks the same. But his shepherd, the ascetic priest, says to him, 'Quite right, my sheep! Somebody must be to blame: but you yourself are this somebody, you yourself alone are to blame for it, *you yourself alone are to blame for yourself.*'" See also *GM*, III, §28.

23. Cf. chapter 6 of Lear 1990. This position on individuality (as a social and psychological achievement) is an essential theme in post-Kantian German philosophy. See Pippin 2000c. The difficulty in discussing the relation between Nietzsche's views and the kind of "recognitional" theories I discuss in the article cited is that, given Nietzsche's diagnosis of the "herd-like" quality of modern society—that is, given his concern with the massive forms of dependence and so conformism required by such societies—he is often loath to say much about the forms of dependence he wants to *promote*. (It is a misleading aspect of many conventional readings that the interpreters assume that Nietzsche is wholly uninterested in such dependencies.) The

the question of whether our threshold in accepting our natural situation of ignorance and suffering has come to be significantly lowered in bourgeois Europe, and he is clearly worried that it has sunk far too low, that we have lost the capacity to feel any self-contempt at our animal status.

The details of this famous genealogy would take us far afield. It is well known that Nietzsche believes that the interpretation of suffering provided by "morality"—that the reason for suffering was the subject's own sinfulness—actually succeeded for a while in creating the conditions of commitment, sacrifice, and dedication, but it exacted far too high a price. It thus ultimately left us "an outpost of discontented, arrogant, and nasty creatures" (*GM*, III, §11, 90) and led us into nihilism. What is important, though, is how frequently Nietzsche tries to show that any sort of self-determined and self-aware pursuit of a goal is both an enormously difficult and quite a fragile collective historical achievement, and one not at all necessarily linked to the Christian and liberal-Enlightenment versions. Accordingly, any philosophical attempt to treat the problems of agency, freedom, and responsibility as abstract metaphysical problems is bound to be merely a kind of game, the rules for which just express a fantasy, or what we need to believe about ourselves at some time. Also, anyone claiming that any of this account shows that we are therefore "unfree wills" or "determined" commits the same mistake and is simply implicitly proposing another ideal, a claim inevitably intertwined with a normative view of what it is to lead a life, either one with some historical resonance, some chance at inspiring a kind of life, or not. (The latest version of the ascetic priest, the modern scientists and their enlightened following, believes this about the beauty or utility of "truth," as much truth as possible. In the second essay of the *Genealogy*, Nietzsche expresses his by now familiar reservations.)

In sum, "with the advent of an animal soul turned against itself, taking sides against itself, something so new, deep, unheard of, enigmatic, contradictory, and full of futurity had come into being that the character of the earth was thereby essentially changed" (*GM*, II, §16, 62, T).

---

theme is mostly available indirectly in remarks about friendship, loneliness, and in Zarathustra's public activities, the consequences of Zarathustra's original reason for coming down from the mountain: "I love man."

VII.

The best example of what I have been talking about occurs in paragraph 300 of *The Gay Science*. Nietzsche first claims that the necessary preconditions for modern science were the "magicians, alchemists, astrologers and witches," because their "promises and pretensions" *"had to create [schaffen mussten]* a thirst, hunger, and taste for *hidden and forbidden* powers," and that much more had to be promised than could be delivered so that this frustration would sustain the scientific enterprise until, much later, the promise could be fulfilled in the "realm of knowledge." Then, in comments on religion, he goes so far as to say that man had to *learn* even to "experience a hunger and thirst for himself," and so to learn to "find satisfaction and fullness in *himself.*" Religious ways of life, in other words, gave human desire a form and a goal; made it possible for me to experience myself as somehow determinately dissatisfying such that I had to become a self, become who I am. His next remark is the most elliptical, and as is usual with Nietzschean imagery like this, it seems to try to create the very thing it describes; an aspiration to meaning, an insistence that there *be* more to understand and that we need to understand it in order to lead a life. "Did Prometheus first have to *imagine* [*wähnen*] having *stolen* light and pay for it before he could finally discover that he had created light *by desiring light*, and that not only man but also *god* was the work of *his own* hands and had been clay in his hands? All mere images of the sculptor—no less than delusion [*Wahn*], theft, the Caucasus, the vulture, and the whole tragic *Prometheia* those who know?" (*GS*, §300, 170). *Prometheus created the light by desiring it* is the phrase that says it all. The lack he experienced was created and sustained by virtue of his action; the lack was not its occasion, and the determinate meaning of what happened—the injustice of Zeus, the meaning of Prometheus's suffering—represent extensions and consequences of the kind of gap he opened up and held open; the enigmatic meaning that he creates by his act and that he promises to be able to explain. This states in an unusually compressed way the idea often associated with Prometheus in interpretations of the myth—that the existence of human beings is completely gratuitous, as if a contingent gift, not something like the necessary unfolding or expression of a fixed and purposively evolving nature or of a divine providence. The image includes within itself the paradox in this way of thinking—that human being, the sense-maker of suffering, is itself the product of human being, as if the cause of itself; and so it suggests the ominous warning: since there was no "reason" for Prometheus's gift, it could just as easily and contingently be canceled.

These passages are dense and elusive, but we need to remember that the theme in these passages is eros, not will or spontaneous creativity, and that any tentative attempts to inspire a kind of longing can fail, and that it is very hard to understand what kind of erotic promises will get a grip and why. It is also one of the reasons there is little in the way of a programmatic response to nihilism in Nietzsche's texts. The failure of desire and its experiential manifestations in everyday life—boredom, loneliness, and fatigue—are very hard to diagnosis and extremely hard to respond to. (The pathos of romantic failure, the ever-possible sudden disappearance of desire, the role of illusion in sustaining any such romantic desire, and the total impossibility of any rational translation of desire into a calculus of mutual satisfaction are, we have seen, major metaphorical variations on the theme of eros throughout Nietzsche's writings.) And again, the extraordinarily enigmatic metaphors and images used by Nietzsche—the eternal return of the same, the spirit of gravity, the pale criminal, a Zoroastrian prophet, a gay science—all seemed mostly to provoke what he has said we need: "neediness" itself; designed to create the need for interpretation, the *expectation* of meaning, and therewith alone the sustenance of human desire, a new kind of victory led by Nietzsche over our present "weariness with man."

These are hard questions to pursue in the language of philosophy (which Nietzsche still by and large retains), not only because the images are interpretable in so many ways but because they are the sorts of questions addressed more regularly by modern, romantic, and confessional poetry than by philosophy. Many times, in ways that clearly echo Montaigne, Nietzsche suggests that a good deal of the answer depends on *him*, on whether he can portray the heroism and beauty of such futile attempts well enough, can inspire a sense of nobility not dependent on guarantees, payoffs, natural completions, benefits, and probabilities. He offers himself as a unique individual possibility, not an instance of a universal rule but a possible paradigm instance to be imitated. Looked at broadly, of course, the historical answer to Nietzsche's question was clearly negative; the experiment with him at the center did not take, his "truth" could not be successfully incorporated. He did not become a new Socrates, and his cultural and historical impact has been much more as a kind of "dissolving fluid," a value-debunker, an immoralist, than as any prophet for a new form of life.

So, while Nietzsche may have avoided the melancholy of someone interminably mourning the death of God and, to use his earlier term of art, avoided the temptation to return to the tragic pessimism of the Greeks, the positive, erotic side of the project he proposes is only just barely on view and remains merely suggestive, tantalizing in the way he probably intends. This is the last erotic "guidepost" I want to mention, and it can only be mentioned here. In paragraph 276 of *The Gay Science*, he writes:

> I, too, want to say what I wish from myself today and what thought first crossed my heart this year—what thought shall be the reason, warrant and sweetness of the rest of my life! I want to learn more and more to see what is necessary in things as what is beautiful in them—thus I will be one of those who make things beautiful. *Amor fati*: Let that be my love from now on! I do not want to wage war against ugliness. I do not want to accuse; I do not even want to accuse the accusers. Let *looking away* be my only negation! And, all in all and on the whole: some day I want only to be a Yes-sayer! (*GS*, §276, 157)

CHAPTER FOUR

"The Deed Is Everything [*Das Tun ist alles*]"

I.

Nietzsche described all modern moral philosophy, together with its psychological assumptions, as a doomed attempt to cling to the fundamental precepts of Christian morality but without the authorizing force that made the whole system credible—a creator God. He understood this morality as essentially an egalitarian humanism, opposed to all forms of egoism or inequality and one promoting a selfless dedication to an ideal according to which everyone would count equally, as only "one among many," in any reflection on what to do.[1] His own view of this attempt is made very clear in the section "Skirmishes of an Untimely Man" in *Twilight of the Idols*, when he indulges in one of his favorite pastimes, making fun of the English, this time at the expense of George Eliot. "When you give up Christian faith, you pull the rug

1. Despite these family resemblances, Nietzsche does not treat *morality* as a completely univocal term and certainly not as a phenomenon with a single necessary essence. But it is clear that he has a standard form of nineteenth-century Christian morality often in his sights. For a summary of those characteristics, see Geuss 1999, 71.

out from under your right to Christian morality as well. . . . Christianity is a system, a carefully considered, *integrated* view of things. If you break off a main tenet, the belief in God, you smash the whole system along with it" (*TI*, 194).[2]

However, as we have seen several times, Nietzsche considers quite difficult and elusive the question of what it would mean to give up such a "system," what it would be for the victory of "European atheism" to be fully "incorporated" as a new form of life. It is clear that he considers such reactions as melancholy, guilt, or despair on the one hand or, on the other hand, low-minded, cynical bourgeois secularism, both as based on misdiagnoses and as psychologically damaging and unstable forms of life. I have suggested that he considers these alternatives as the sorts of dangers evident in such champions of honesty as Pascal and La Rochefoucauld and that he appears to think only Montaigne succeeded in living a life free of Christian moralism or its aftereffects. (Obviously, *quite* a controversial view of Montaigne and Christianity, especially Montaigne's Christianity, nowadays.)

I am interested, in this chapter, in why Nietzsche thinks we ought to give up another remnant of the Christian system, perhaps the most tenacious of all and the most basic: our belief in the ontologically distinct subject as agent, separable from, supervising, willing into existence, and individually responsible for her particular actions. I am especially interested in what he thinks *giving up such a commitment* would amount to (this chapter) and how we ought to picture a life without such a commitment (in chapters 5 and 6).

To start with, I should recall two features of the interpretation presented in the previous three chapters. The first concerns the "primordiality of psychology" in Nietzsche's works. I have interpreted that to mean the priority and nonreducibility of normative considerations as a condition for the intelligibility of our assertions and our actions. In Nietzsche's language, this amounts to the primordiality of "esteeming"

2. As noted previously, this and many other passages betray an odd kind of Hegelian rationalism in Nietzsche: the view that a form of life demanding such incompatible commitments would become a kind of practical impossibility and require some revolutionary change. There is another side to Nietzsche's account, though, one more "Kuhnean," one might say, wherein the great crisis of the aftermath of European Christianity is that *no one appreciates it as a crisis*, that this incompatibility can easily survive without creating any sort of suffering; we are not ashamed of it.

(valuing, understood primarily as the ability to make and keep promises, etc.) in the possibility of leading a human life. However, such commitments and pledges cannot be made ex nihilo; they occur within ongoing, already norm-governed practices that themselves depend on basic, or depth, commitments, which cannot finally be the implications of other commitments. I have tried to demonstrate that Nietzsche very frequently and throughout his writing career refers to this basic orientation in life in terms of eros and erotic attachment, prereflective and prevolitional, all in a way that manifests his familiarity with the importance of that theme in the Platonic Socrates. This picture of Nietzsche makes very unlikely any view of him as continuing and radicalizing an enlightenment project or as some sort of existentialist, encouraging us simply to have the strength of will to create new, life-affirming values. "What we care about," at a basic level, always already orders the relations of significance and importance in our cognitive (explanatory) concerns and in what we find worthy of striving for. It also means that the heart of his nihilism concern is a historically distinct, collective failure of desire. (Like Heidegger, Nietzsche treats these basic commitments as at least partly accessible and perhaps revisable only in times of contingent, near complete breakdown.)

Second, this view of Nietzsche's work throws into a different light how he means to address such a failure. Since the basic phenomenon of orientation and normative identification occurs largely prevolitionally and prereflectively, Nietzsche's texts are overwhelmingly literary, rhetorically complex, elliptical, and always a matter of adopting personae and "masks," often the mask of a historian or scientist. He appears to believe that this is the only effective way to reach the level of such concerns, and he clearly thinks he has such a chance, in the current historical context of crisis, collapse, boredom, and confusion, a chance of shaming and cajoling us away from commitments that will condemn us to a "last man" or "pale atheist" sort of existence and of inspiring a new desire, a new "tension" of the spirit. The Greeks managed a tragic pessimism, he reasoned from the very beginning of his publications; why can't we do likewise?[3] Hence the importance of these endless pictures and images: truth as a woman, science as gay,

3. As we have seen, he notes that this view may be naive, even hopeless, but he accepts that danger as what he calls his own "type of injustice" (*GS*, §2, 30).

troubadours, Baubo, tomb robbers, seduction, romance, prophets, animals, tightrope walkers, dwarves, beehives, crazy men, sleep, dreams, breeding, blond beasts, a twilight of idols, and on and on. It makes all the difference in the world if, having appreciated this point, we then appreciate that such notions as "the will to power" and "the eternal return of the same" *belong on this list,* are not independent philosophical explanations of the meaning of the list. It is not an accident that Nietzsche often introduces *these* notions with the same hypothetical indirectness that he uses for the other images.

II.

But that would be an independent book on Nietzsche's style (a book we still need). For the moment, we must turn our attention to by far the most important, the foundational claim in modern moral psychology—belief in "that little changeling, the 'subject'" (*GM*, I, §13, 28). As is well known, in his *Genealogy,* Nietzsche approached this issue by offering a historical and psychological narrative about the origin of the notion of such a subject. His story purported to show why a certain type (the weak) would try to justify its position relative to the stronger type by portraying the master's expression of strength as "evil" and the situation of the defeated slave as "good." This, in turn, if it was to be an effective *condemnation* (rather than a mere report of the facts), had to go one step further than characterizing those who end up "by nature" as such overpowering types, one step further than just characterizing the weak type, those who happen in fact to be meek, humble, sympathetic to the suffering of others, and so forth. The real genius of the slave rebellion, according to Nietzsche, lies in its going beyond a simple inversion of value types and in the creation of a new way of thinking about human beings: the creation of a subject "behind" the actual deed, one who could have acted to express his strength (or virtuous weakness) *or not* and who thus can be condemned and held individually and completely responsible for his voluntary oppression of others, even as the slave can be praised for his supposedly voluntary and so praiseworthy withdrawal from the struggle. Nietzsche's psychological narrative points to a distinct motive that explains this ideological warfare and invention—his phrase is, "thanks to the counterfeit and self-deception of *impotence*" (*GM*, I, §13, 27)—and draws a conclusion about the realization of this motive, such that the slave can act, "as if the weakness of the weak were itself—I mean its *essence*, its effect, its whole unique, unavoidable, irredeemable reality—a voluntary achievement, something wanted, chosen, a *deed*, an *accomplishment*. This type of man *needs* to believe in an unbiased 'subject' with freedom of choice, because he has an instinct of self-preservation and self-affirmation" (ibid.).[4] However, as in many other cases, Nietzsche is not content merely to ascribe these psychological motivations to the originators of some moral code. Even if the slaves had such a need, establishing that would not of itself establish the further claim that this slavishly motivated commitment is actually false, *necessarily* self-deceived. The reaction could clearly both be motivated by ressentiment and nevertheless involve a true or an objective moral evaluation. Nietzsche clearly realizes this and certainly wants to establish that further point. He suggests how he intends to demonstrate it in a famous simile proposed in *On the Genealogy of Morals* (I, §13), just before the passages cited above, by yet another "picture argument." The main element of the picture is stated right after another, after he notes that there is nothing surprising or even objectionable in the fact that "little lambs" insist that the greatest evil is "bird of prey [*Raubvögeln*]" behavior and that the highest good is little lamb behavior. Nietzsche goes on:

> It is just as absurd to ask strength *not* to express itself as strength, *not* to be a desire to overcome, crush, become master, to be a thirst for enemies, resistance and triumphs, as it is to ask weakness to express itself as strength. . . . And just as the common people separate lightning

4. The experience of the two differing motivations cited in these two passages is obviously supposed to be linked. Nietzsche appears to assume that the experience of such impotence itself is, if confronted unadorned, unbearable in some way, threatens one's very "self-preservation," requires a "self-affirmation" if one is to continue to lead a life. Hence the "self-deception," the compensatory belief that one's "impotence" is actually an achievement to be admired. In sum, this invention of a subject (or soul) independent of and "behind" its deeds is "that sublime self-deception" that "construe[s] weakness itself as freedom, and their particular mode of existence as an *accomplishment*" (*GM*, I, §13, 27). This is all linked to Nietzsche's view of self-reflexive subjectivity as a reactive phenomenon, a response to suffering and the problem of its meaning. See the discussion in chapter 3.

from its flash, and take the latter to be a *deed*, something performed
by a subject, which is called lightning, popular morality separates
strength from the manifestation of strength, as though there were
an indifferent substratum behind the strong person which had the
freedom to manifest strength or not. But there is no such substratum;
there is no "being" behind the deed, its effect and what becomes of
it; "the doer" is invented as an afterthought,—the deed is everything.
(*GM*, I, §13, 26, T)

This denial of a subject behind the deed and responsible for it is so
sweeping that it immediately raises a problem for Nietzsche, something
actually very hard to picture. It is the same question that would arise for
anyone attacking our commonsense psychological view that holds that
a subject's intention (normally understood as a desire for an end, accompanied by a belief about means, or a subject's deciding or willing or
committing to act for some purpose or end) must stand both "behind"
and "before" some activity in order for the event to be distinguished *as
a deed at all,* as something *done* by someone. We must be able to appeal
to such a subject's intention in order to be able to distinguish between
event types such as "someone volunteering for a risky mission" from
event types such as steel rusting or water running downhill or a bird
singing.[5] It is "behind" the deed in the sense that observers see only the
movements of bodies—say, someone stepping out from a line of men—
and must infer to some intending subject in order to understand and
explain both what happened and why the action occurred. If there "is"
just the deed, we tend to think, stepping out of line *is* just body movement, metaphysically like the wind knocking over a lamp (or perhaps
a gust of wind pushing someone forward just as volunteers are called
for). A subject's intention is "before" the deed because that commonsense psychological explanation typically points to such a prior intention as the cause of the act; what best answers the question, "Why did
that occur?" Or more normally, "Why are you doing that?"

5. The identification of such a prior condition is, in Wittgenstein's famous words,
what would distinguish my arm going up from my raising my arm. (The mistake, for
both Nietzsche and Wittgenstein, lies in thinking that fulfillment of this condition
must be an inner mental state or occurrence, understood as privately owned by an
individual and causally responsible for a bodily movement.)

III.

And here again we confront the problem of a naturalist interpretation of Nietzsche. As we have frequently seen, Nietzsche is understandably often described as a naturalist, perhaps a psychological naturalist in his account of moral institutions. On the assumption that naturalism holds that there are only material objects in space and time (perhaps just the entities and properties referred to by the most advanced modern sciences) and that all explanation is scientific explanation, essentially subsumption under a scientific law, it is unlikely that Nietzsche accepts *this* sort of naturalism, especially the latter condition. In *On the Genealogy of Morals* (II, §12), he complains about the "mechanistic senselessness" of modern science, and he calls the view of lawlike regularity a "democratic idiosyncrasy" (*GM*, II, §12, 52). But many people think he accepts at least the former or ontological condition and that such acceptance may partly explain what is going on in the denial of any separate soul in essay I, paragraph 13—that is, that Nietzsche mostly means to deny "free will."

Nietzsche's descriptions of the strong and the weak in essay I, paragraph 13, have indeed already expressed the antivoluntarist view that the strong can "do nothing else but" express their strength. He seems to treat the commonsense psychology just sketched as essentially and wholly derivative from the slave or ultimately Christian compensatory fantasy of self-determining subjects and a "could have done otherwise" sense of freedom. (How there could even be such a thing as a "compensatory fantasy"—that is, how there could be such a thing as self-deceit—is the subject of the next chapter.) This all does make it tempting to regard him as indifferent to the distinction between ordinary natural events and actions and as perfectly content to consider the "reactive force" most responsible for the slave rebellion—ressentiment—as one of the many natural psychological forces or drives in the world that we will need to appeal to in order to account for various social and political appearances. All this by contrast with a separate subject that could act or not, depending on what it decides. We could interpret essay I, paragraph 13, as only denying the possibility of this metaphysically free subject behind the deed and attribute to Nietzsche a broadly consistent naturalism. (Nietzsche certainly believes that the free will picture *is* a fantasy [*BGE*, §19, 21; *TI*, §7 of "The Four Great Errors," 181], and in *On the Genealogy of Morals,* essay I, paragraph 13, he obviously thinks that the classic picture of a commanding will and the resultant action give us, paradoxically and unacceptably, *two* actions, not one,[6] and that it pushes the basic question of origin back yet again.)

The trouble with proceeding very far in this direction is that Nietzsche does not seem interested in merely naturalizing all talk of motives, goals, intentions, and aversions; he denies that whole model of behavior, "root and branch." The passages just quoted do not appear to leave room for *corporeal* states causing various body movements, as if, for example, a subject's socially habituated fear for his reputation (where fear is understood as some sort of corporeal state) were "behind" his stepping out of line and acting in a way he knew would count for others as volunteering. If that model were adopted, we would still be pointing to some determinate causal factor "behind" and "before" the deed. The "lightning" simile is unequivocal, though, and we would not be following its suggestion if we merely substituted a material *substance* (such as the brain or brain states) for an immaterial soul. Moreover, such a naturalist account relies on the material continuity through time of some identical substance in order to attribute to it various manifestations and expressions as interconnected properties. If there were no substance or subject of any kind behind or underlying various different events, it is hard to see how we might individuate these expressions of force, and even if we could, how we might distinguish a universe of episodic, atomistic events from the world that Nietzsche himself refers to, a world of *slaves, masters, institutions, priests,* and so on. He nowhere seems inclined to treat such a world as arbitrarily grouped collections of force-events (grouped together by whom or what?), as if these were either "becoming master" events or "becoming subdued by" events, and so forth. We thus still need a credible interpretation of the following claim: "But there is no *such substratum; there is no "being" behind doing, effecting, becoming; "the doer" is merely a fiction added to the deed—the deed is everything*" (*GM*, I, §13, 26). Materialist or naturalist bloody-mindedness is not going to help. And so we need to think again about what "the deed is everything" might amount to.

6. Bernard Williams 1994, 242. Searle (2001) multiplies matters even more, adding as an action our persistence in the deed once undertaken.

IV.

The difficulty is quite serious for Nietzsche. If we accept that there is *no* doer behind the deed, we will have also made it very difficult to understand the whole of Nietzsche's own attack on the moral psychology of Christian morality, since he himself appears to rely on a traditional understanding of act descriptions (that the act is individuated as an act mainly by reference to the agent's intentions), and he invokes a complex picture of unconscious motives, operative and motivating, but inaccessible as such to the agents involved. (Not to mention that we shall be left with little coherent to say about Nietzsche's claim in paragraph 23 of *Beyond Good and Evil* that "from now on, psychology is again the path to the fundamental problems.") Values cannot be said to simply "grow" organically, given some sort of context. For one thing, as we have repeatedly seen, we must *make* ourselves into creatures capable of keeping promises, and this requires many centuries of commitment, punishment, perseverance, and so the unmistakable exercise of subjectivity. It seems a question-begging evasion to gloss all such appeals as really about "what happens *to* us," what madness befalls us, in situations of subjection. There would be little reason to take Nietzsche seriously if he were out to make what Bernard Williams has called the "uninviting" claim that "we never really do anything, that no events are actions."[7]

We might do better, I want to suggest, to appreciate first that the surface meaning of the claims made in essay I, paragraph 13, remains quite elusive. As he had pointed out in essay II, paragraph 12, the notion of an "activity" functions as a "fundamental concept" in what Nietzsche himself claims, and he insists in that passage on a contrast between such an activity and the "mechanistic senselessness" of the ordinary modern scientific worldview. We thus need to return to essay I, paragraph 13, and appreciate that Nietzsche is not denying that *there is* a subject of the deed. He is just asserting that it is not *separate*, distinct from the activity itself; it is "in" the deed. He is not denying that strength "*expresses* itself" in acts of strength. He is in fact asserting just that, that there is such an *expression*, and so appears to be relying on a notion of expression, rather than intentional causality, to understand

7. Williams 1994, 241.

how the doer is in the deed. ("To demand of strength that it should *not* express itself as strength" is the expression he uses. He does not say, "There are just strength-events." There is still some sort of dyadic logic to his claim.) That—the appeal to expression—is quite an important clue. He is not denying, in other words, that there is a deed, and that it must be distinguishable from any mere event. He maintains that distinction. Indeed, there are frequently, throughout his work, other such metaphorical expressions that are both striking and somewhat mysterious as well as indications of how important the issue is to Nietzsche. Here is a typical example from *Thus Spoke Zarathustra*: "I wish *your* self were in the deed like the mother is in the child. Let that be *your* word on virtue" (*TSZ*, 74).[8] This suggests a very different relation between self and deed than cause and effect, but we would still have to know first *how*, for Nietzsche, a mother can be said to be "in" her child before we can appreciate what is being suggested, and that is not initially clear. One thing it suggests immediately, though, is quite striking. A mother both "sees" herself in the child and yet acknowledges the child's own independence as a person in her own right, suggesting that once we "launch" a deed, it takes on a life of its own in the world (something obviously paradoxical, given the lightning/flash image), taken up by others in ways we could not have anticipated, perhaps manifesting aspects of our own character that we would not have anticipated. The image further deflates any notion of a strict individual ownership of the deed, even as it proposes another sort of attachment to our deeds as somehow still "our own" even if independent of us and from any individual causal agency.

Put in terms of the image we have been exploring, we cannot say "there are only deeds," not agents, just as we cannot say that the flash is *just* an electrical discharge in the air. Clearly, a certain *sort* of meteorological event is "expressed," and so a phenomenally identical "flash" might not be lightning but could be artificially produced. It would be

---

8. Christa Davis Acampora (forthcoming) suggests a number of interesting variations on this theme, well worth taking up. I don't think, though, that this passage and others undermine what remains a distinction for Nietzsche between events in which a doer is expressed, or "in" the deed, and events that are mere natural occurrences. His account of the slave revolt, or self-deceit, or ressentiment, and on the practical teleology of action, all, it seems to me, require some account of practical intentionality, however distinctive and nondyadic.

a phenomenally identical event, but not lightning. Its distinctness depends on *what* it is expressing.

In order to understand this claim about there being a doer, but "in" the deed, it might help to realize that Nietzsche is not alone in this insistence. There is a kind of brotherhood of modern anti-Cartesians, let us say, philosophers united in their opposition to metaphysical dualism, to a picture of mind shut up in itself and its own ideas and so in an unsolvable skeptical dilemma about the real world, and opposed as well to the notion of autonomous, identifiable subjects, whose internally and transparently accessible intentions and determinate acts of willing best identify and explain distinct sorts of events in the world, actions. There is a range in such a group, including Nietzsche and Wittgenstein and Heidegger, as well as an early member, Hegel.[9]

What has been called this "expressivist" notion of action, as opposed to an intentionalist or a causal account,[10] is quite relevant here for understanding how Nietzsche could appear to deny any standard picture of agency and of normal volitional responsibility and yet still speak of *actions* and of the expression of a subject in the action, indeed *wholly* in the action. The main similarity turns on what might be called an "inseparability thesis" about intention and action and a corresponding claim about the impossibility of isolating a subject's determinate intention, the claim that the determinate meaning of such an intention cannot be made out if isolated from a much larger complex of social and historical factors.

9. Baruch Spinoza probably deserves pride of place as the first. I discuss the distinctly Hegelian take on this issue in chapter 6 of Pippin 2008a. I hope the fuller account there of the expressivist position makes contact with the compelling questions raised about that position by Anderson (forthcoming). The claim in question, which I am arguing is Nietzsche's claim as well, is that there are ways of answering the central phenomenological question—in what way can an agent come to recognize herself in her deed?—without limiting such a connection to a causal agency. I can recognize myself in the deed if the deed can be said to "express" me, a claim that obviously needs a great deal more unpacking. Hegel believes that there are social conditions for this possibility, conditions of social dependence, and as noted before, while there are indications that Nietzsche recognizes the importance of such a condition, he does not much develop it.

10. See especially Taylor 1975, 1985c, and 1985a.

According to the first, or inseparability, thesis, intention formation and articulation are always temporally fluid, altering and transformable "on the go," as it were, as events in a project unfold. I may start out engaged in a project, understanding my intention as X, and over time, come to understand that this first characterization was not really an accurate or a full description of what I intended; it must have been Y, or later perhaps Z. And there is no way to confirm the certainty of one's "real" purpose except *in* the deed actually performed. My subjective construal at any time before or during the deed has no privileged authority. The deed *alone* can show one who one is, what one is actually committed to, despite what one sincerely avows. This means that the act description cannot be separated from this mutable intention, since, as the intention comes into a kind of focus, what it is I take myself to be doing can also alter. That is, we should understand successful action as a continuous and temporally extended, everywhere mutable translation or expression of inner into outer, but not as an isolated and separated determinate inner struggling for expression in imperfect material. Our original avowals of intention (even just to ourselves) are only provisional starting points, formulated with incomplete knowledge of circumstances and consequences. We have to understand the end and the reason for pursuing it as both constantly transformed, such that what I end up with, what I actually did, is all that can count fully as my intention realized or expressed.

Likewise, there is a common "nonisolatability" thesis in such expressivist accounts. According to this view, attending only to a specific intention as both accounting for why the act occurred and what is actually undertaken, distorts what is necessary for a full explanation of an action. In the first place, the conditions under which one *would* regard an intention as justifying an action (or not) have to be part of the picture, too, and this shifts our attention to the person's character and then to his life history and even to a community as a whole or to a tradition. We have to have all that in view before the adoption of a specific intention can itself make sense. Indeed, this assumption is already on view from the start in Nietzsche's genealogy, since he treats the unequal distribution of social power as an essential element in understanding "what the slavish type was attempting." The psychology that Nietzsche announces as "the queen of the sciences" is also a social and historical psychology.

While on the standard intentionalist model, the criterion for success of an action amounts to whether the originally held purpose was in fact achieved, on this different model, "success" is much more complicated. I must be able to "see myself" in the deed (sometimes the surprising, unexpected deed) as actually performed, see it as an expression of me (in a sense not restricted to my singular intention), but also such that what *I* understand is being attempted and realized is also what *others* understand. I haven't *performed the action*, haven't volunteered for the mission, if nothing I do is so understood by others as *that* act.[11] This social dimension is often ignored in Nietzsche interpretations in favor of some heroic individualism, but a brief look at the complex issue of Zarathustra's relation with, especially his failures with, his audience should make the point immediately.[12]

To put the matter more straightforwardly, if I start out to write a poem, I might find that it does not go as I expected and think this is because the material "resists" my execution, my inner poem, and so what I get is a "poorly expressed poem." This is a very misleading picture on this account, as misleading as the commanding will of *Beyond Good and* Evil, paragraph 19. The poem is a perfect expression of what your intention and ability *turned out to be*. To ask for a better poem is to ask for *another* one, for the formation and execution of another intention. If the poem failed, everything has failed. It (the expression of what has turned out to be the "intended poem") just ended up being a bad poem, not a bad expression of a good poem. As Nietzsche keeps insisting, our egos are wedded to the latter account; but the former correctly expresses what happened.

Now, philosophically, a great deal more needs to be said before this understanding of "the doer *in* the deed" could be defended. The

11. We could use Brandom's pragmatic terminology (1994) to make this point and say that for an action to be a successful action, the commitments I undertake must be those also attributed to me by others, and that we thus must make room for the original uncertainty "for me" about precisely *what* I am undertaking and the unacceptability of any one-sided answer (as in: "*just* what others attribute to me").

12. See Pippin 1988 for a fuller discussion of this point. As noted in earlier remarks, there is not a lot of material in Nietzsche to work with on this point, and Zarathustra's dramatic enactment of his own dependence in his various ascents and descents, and in the problematic relation he establishes (and then breaks) with his disciples, is a rich source, if also elusive.

anti-Cartesian and broadly anti-Christian account asks for something quite unusual. These passages in Nietzsche seem to be asking us to relocate our attention when trying to understand an action, render a deed intelligible, from attention to a prior event or mental state (the formation of and commitment to an intention, whether a maxim, or desire-plus-belief, etc.) to (or at least also to) "what lies *deeper* in the deed itself" and is expressed in it. (Where *deeper* does not mean already there, hidden in the depths, but not yet fully formed and realized.)[13] Rather, the interpretive task focuses on a continuing expression or translation of the subject into the actuality of the deed, and conversely, our translation *back* into "who the person is."[14]

This can all sound counterintuitive because it seems obvious that the final deed may not express the agent simply because some contingency intervened and prevented the full realization (thus reinstituting a "separation" between the subject in itself and the deed that actually resulted, shaped as it so often is by external circumstances and events). Or we easily accept that if someone did something unknowingly and innocently, he cannot be said to be properly "in" the deed, even though the deed came about because of him and no one else, as when someone genuinely does not know that he is revealing a secret and does so, but guiltlessly, we want to say.[15]

---

13. As with the "gay science" discussion in chapter 2, there is nothing behind the deed, the appearances, until "after the deed," when the subject's intention can be "seen" for the first time.

14. Cf. *AC*: "A virtue needs to be our *own* invention, our *own* most personal need and self-defence.... Whatever is not a condition for life *harms* it" (*AC*, 9).

15. The issues are quite complicated and cannot be pursued here. The most difficult question is much more immediate: should not Nietzsche be aware that, by eliminating as nonsensical the idea that appears to be a necessary condition for a deed being a deed—a subject's individual causal responsibility for the deed's occurring—he has eliminated *any* way of properly understanding the notion of *responsibility*, or that he has eliminated even a place for criticism of an agent? If strength is not at all "free" to be weak, is not free to express that strength in any way other than by "a desire to overcome, a desire to throw down, a desire to become master, a thirst for enemies and resistances and triumphs," in *what* "responsibility sense" *is* the agent *in* the deed if not "causally" (*GM*, I, §13)? A plant's life cycle might be said to be "expressed" in its various stages, but, as we have seen, Nietzsche rejects such a reductionist reading; he shows no indication of wanting to eliminate his "fundamental concept," activity. I discuss the "intervening contingencies" problem as these

Now, it is true that sometimes Nietzsche seems content with a kind of typological determinism. People just *belong* to some type or other (whether biological or socially formed), and some just *are* weak, base, vengeful, and ugly; others are strong, noble, generous, and beautiful. (Cf. *BGE*, §265.) There is no way to justify these distinctions; that is the "Socratic" trick that the former group tries to play on the latter. The whole point is that you have to *be* a member of the latter group to appreciate the distinction; everything starts from that point. But actually Nietzsche's own evaluations are not so tied to this fixed typology. About the weak he says "The history of mankind would be far too stupid a thing if it had not had the spirit of the powerless injected into it" (*GM*, I, §7, 17). Likewise, he certainly seems to be criticizing the nobility by contrast when he says "It was on the foundation of this *essentially dangerous* form of human existence, the priestly form, that man first became an *interesting animal* and that the human soul first acquired *depth* in a higher sense and became *evil*—and there are the two basic forms of man's superiority, hitherto, over other beasts!" (*GM*, I, §6, 16, T). Such passages suggest a radical flexibility and indeterminateness in the normative value of such distinctions, an unpredictability in what they "turn out" to mean, as if Nietzsche thinks that such oppositions look one way in one context, another in another context. That raises the question of how this variation works, how this interpretive struggle is to be understood, and what its relation might be to the psychological struggle.

Nietzsche has a great many things to say about this hermeneutical warfare, but we should note that his remarks confirm attributing the "nonisolatability" thesis to him, as noted above, and the second "success" condition for actions as understood on this alternate model. Not only is the determinate meaning of a subject's intention not a matter of inner perception and sincerity but a function in some way of a certain social context, especially a struggle for control of the agenda in such a society, but also "*what* is going on" in such a context is itself constantly contested among the participants. As he put it in the passage I cited

---

appear in Hegel's similar expressivist account in Pippin 2008a, chapter 6. (There is a separate and narrower concept of legal responsibility, and that may be all we need. That is, Did the agent do it, bring it about? Did he know what he was doing? Was he coerced? If the answers are yes, yes, and no, he was responsible.)

in an earlier chapter, "that everything that occurs in the organic world consists of *overpowering*, *dominating*, and in their turn, overpowering and dominating consist of re-interpretation, adjustment in the process of which their former 'meaning' and 'purpose' must necessarily be obscured or completely obliterated" (*GM*, II, §12, 51).

He makes the same sort of point about the variability and contestability of the various understandings of punishment (*GM*, II, §14) and notes that even the noble man *needs* the appropriate enemies if his actions are to have the meaning he sees expressed in them (*GM*, I, §10). In such cases, "the subject" is not absent; he is "out there" in his deeds, but *the deeds are "out there," too*, multiply interpretable, and that means, in Nietzsche's understanding, that they can be in multiple ways "appropriated" by others. These interpretations are themselves already expressions of various types that cannot be isolated from historical time and from the contestations of their own age. We have already good reason to be cautious of interpreters who think that there must be something appealed to, underlying Nietzsche's account, as a kind of criterion: "life," and/or "the will to power," to cite the most frequent candidates. If life must also turn against itself to be life, and if we don't know what really counts as having established power, or even *what power is*, we have only returned again to a social struggle about the meaning of deeds. In other words, if the most important deed is the legislation of values, what *actually* is legislated cannot be fixed by the noble man's strength of resolve *alone* or guaranteed by his "pathos of distance." There is a difference between actually legislating values, that is, succeeding in doing so, and, on the other hand, engaging in a fantasy of self and value creation.

V.

I want to conclude this part of the discussion with one last psychological issue, by returning briefly to the main intuitive difficulty created by *On the Genealogy of Morals*, essay I, paragraph 13, especially about responsibility. We should note, that is, Nietzsche's own response to the responsibility question—how, in his picture of how an agent is wholly in the deed, not separate from it, such reactions as regret, sorrow about what one did, might be understood.

Not surprisingly (given their similarities on so many issues), Nietzsche turns to Spinoza to make his point, and his remarks in essay II, paragraph 15, of *On the Genealogy of Morals* are perfectly consistent with and, I think, confirm the position attributed to him above. He muses that Spinoza might have one afternoon asked himself, given that there is no free will or separate subject underlying the deed in Spinoza's own system, what could remain in that system of the *morsus conscientiae*, the sting of conscience. This is the very intuitive, or commonsense, question we have posed above. Nietzsche first appeals to Spinoza by making his own attempt at a "becoming master" of Spinoza, offering his own "fresh interpretation" of Spinoza, and announcing "The world, for Spinoza, had returned to that state of innocence in which it had lain before the invention of the bad conscience" (*GM*, II, §15, 56). But then he notes that Spinoza reinvented this *morsus conscientiae* in his *Ethics*.[16] "'The opposite of *gaudium*,' he finally said to himself,—'a sadness accompanied by the recollection of a past event which turned out contrary to expectation.' . . . For millennia, wrongdoers overtaken by punishment have felt *no different than Spinoza* with regard to their 'offence': 'something has gone unexpectedly wrong here,' *not* 'I ought not to have done that'" (ibid.).

So disappointment that I was not who I thought I was, sadness at what was expressed "in" the deed, replaces guilt, or the sort of guilt that depends on the claim that I could have done otherwise. Indeed, it is a kind of regret that depends on my not really having had the option to do otherwise; or at least that counterfactual option, on this view, is like considering the possibility that I might not have been me, a fanciful and largely irrelevant speculation, a mere thought experiment.

None of this settles the many other questions raised by Nietzsche's position: What are the conditions necessary for rightly identifying what it was that I did? What role do the judgments of others properly play in that assessment? Deeds, even understood as expressions rather than caused results, conflict, express incompatible, if also provisional and changing, purposes. How do we, as nonparticipants, understand and even evaluate such conflicts? Are not our interpretations the expressions of *current* contestations, and if so, what would count as success, as prevailing now? How much of "who I am" can be said to be

16. Spinoza, *Ethics* III, Definitions XVI, XVII, XVIII.

expressed in the deed? How might we distinguish important discoveries about myself that I had not known and would have denied, from trivial or irrelevant revelations? If whatever it is that is expressed in such deeds is not a stable core or substantial self, neither as an individual soul nor as a substantial type, what could form the basis of the temporal story that would link these manifestations and transformations?

These are difficult questions, but, I have tried to show, they are the right sort of questions raised by Nietzsche's remarks in *On the Genealogy of Morals*, essay I, paragraph 13, and they are very different from questions about metaphysical forces, naturalized psychologies, instinct theories, or existential, groundless choices, leaps into the abyss.

CHAPTER FIVE

The Psychological Problem of Self-Deception

I.

Our problem has been Nietzsche's apparent claim that psychology, not metaphysics or epistemology, should be understood ("now," "again") as playing a role very much like what Aristotle called first philosophy. Such an inquiry has required two obvious elements. First, we needed some sense of what Nietzsche meant by psychology and especially by psychological explanation. I suggested that the "French moralists" were his main model for such an enterprise. Second, we needed to understand why he thought answers to such questions were in some sense logically prior to, say, truth claims about nature, or philosophical claims about being qua being, or direct questions about the best human life, and so forth. That led us to the centrality of value and valuing in Nietzsche's project and to his unusual account of how things come to matter and cease to matter to human beings. His remarks on love and desire were central here. Along the way I have tried to indicate how this interpretation makes a difference in the way we interpret a number of important Nietzschean claims, especially his treatment of subjectivity and agency. I propose now to continue this

latter discussion by focusing on two of the most important instances of
Nietzschean psychological analysis at work: in this chapter his crucial
account of self-deception (which will link up explicitly with the last
chapter's treatment of agency) and in the next his appeal to the value
of self-overcoming.

II.

We can start again with what Nietzsche appears to say, what he is
often taken to mean. He frequently contrasts what he calls "consciousness" with what he calls "instincts." A typical claim can be found in the
second-edition preface to *The Gay Science* and in its first book. From
the preface: "The unconscious disguise of physiological needs under
the cloaks of the objective, ideal, purely spiritual goes frighteningly
far. . . . Behind the highest value judgments that have hitherto guided
the history of thought are concealed misunderstandings of the physical constitution" (*GS*, preface, 5). And from paragraph 11 of the first
book: "Consciousness is the latest development of the organic, and
hence also its most unfinished and unrobust feature. . . . One thinks it
constitutes the kernel of man, what is abiding, eternal, ultimate, most
original in him. . . . This ridiculous overestimation and misapprehen-
sion of consciousness had the very useful consequence that an all-
too-rapid development of consciousness was prevented. . . . The task
of assimilating knowledge and making it instinctive is still quite new"
(*GS*, §11, 37). Or in book 4 of *The Gay Science*: "Your judgment, 'that is
right' has a prehistory in your drives, inclinations, aversions, experiences, and what you have failed to experience" (*GS*, §335, 187). These
are the sorts of claims about the doubled nature of human psychology that lie behind many of Nietzsche's best-known positions: that
philosophy is in actuality the personal psychological confession of its
author, or most famously that allegiance to the Christian religion was
not originally and is not now motivated by a genuine belief in revelation or for any consciously held reasons and motives or religious
experience, even though the devout may sincerely believe this. Rather,
the original Christian movement was carried out by those who were
by psychological type weak and slavish, chafing under the authority

of Roman masters, but who (these slaves) nevertheless "creatively" found a way to rebel. But that rebellion was motivated not by what they consciously (and sincerely) ascribed to themselves but, in some way beneath the level of conscious awareness, by resentment and a profound hatred of their masters. (So, in Nietzsche's paradoxical way, the fact that the doctrinal content of the new religion required "love of one's enemies" is a strategy in a reaction motivated by a form of bitter hatred of those enemies, ressentiment.) Thus they were able to interpret their weakness and cowardice as piety and humility and to condemn their masters' self-confidence and independence as sinful vanity and egoism.

Many interpreters of Nietzsche see this account as one example among many of a general claim and the general psychologically reductionist approach that we have been discussing throughout. According to this view, Nietzsche held that human conduct was always and everywhere best explained by reference to basic human drives that determined behavior independent of conscious assessments and motives, which were always ex post facto rationalizations. Indeed, such behavior was determined by one master-drive, the will to power, some sort of always present but in some sense or other "unconscious" drive or conatus toward power, understood in the broadest human sense as not being subject to the will of others (or even any other thing or animal or force) but being able to subject others to one's own will. (It is not easy for commentators who take this line to explain exactly what Nietzsche might mean by *determine*, given that he is quite skeptical about causal explanations and that he wants to distinguish his claim from any doctrine of either a free or an unfree will.) There are many ways of putting the point, but in the popular mind, this picture of the single ferocious drive to which all others are subservient or even reducible is the heart of what is taken to be the Nietzschean claim about an omnipresent, remorseless, pitiless, brute drive to domination, apparent everywhere, especially in activities and practices that appear to be motivated by just the opposite intentions. And some commentators go further still and, inspired by the fragments of what they believe Nietzsche planned as his magnum opus, *Der Wille zur Macht* (*The Will to Power*), they see such a "force" in the organic world as universally present, not just in humans but also in animals, plants, cells, and so forth.

III.

But the first thing we need to note is that Nietzsche often goes to great lengths to make clear that he is *not* merely contrasting, on the one hand, the pretensions of the conscious mind that it can explain what an agent is doing by reference to consciously held reasons with what, on the other hand, should count as the real explicans of such action, somatic basic instinctual drives that so incline us toward a particular course of action as to be irresistible and that direct behavior in a way independent of conscious intentionality. As we shall see, there is little doubt that Nietzsche understands ressentiment-like motivation as a thoroughly psychological and even an intentional phenomenon. And it is also apparent that he is not talking about anything as straightforward and common as knowing hypocrisy. That is, he also says that these drives or instincts function in a distinctly unacknowledged way; they are *hidden*, not merely unnoticed or beyond conscious control or acknowledged and motivating but hypocritically denied. This is a strange enough claim. If I am hungry or thirsty or angry at my masters or seized by romantic passion, this all hardly happens behind the back of consciousness; I am quite intensely aware of being hungry or angry or resentful or aroused. And if I am genetically determined to crave sweets, that hardly seems a factor that, because nonconscious, should be said to be *hidden*. Presumably, while I might interpret my craving as an intense interest in the variety of life, I am certainly aware of a desire to eat sweet things. *It* is not "hidden." (I can come to know such a truth and try to hide *that*, the truth, but that reintroduces many of the paradoxes we will soon see.) Things are even more complicated because Nietzsche also makes clear that he thinks *we* are the ones who do the hiding. Moreover, if I am moved to utter some words, initiate some body actions, bestow loyalty on comrades, and so forth, in a complex set of actions determined or caused by drives of which I am unaware—if, in effect, *I am rebelling and do not know that I am rebelling*—it is hard to see how I could experience any psychological satisfaction of the nonconscious desire from rebelling. Drives must have intentional content, in other words, and that means that if they are to explain behavior, they cannot determine the psychological from "outside the psychological," as extrapsychological phenomena. And this last point (which I will try to explain more in a moment) is in some tension with the conventional view summarized above.

That is, while such claims have become staples of any summary of Nietzsche, the logic or psychological dynamic he is assuming is clearly quite unusual. Real motives, according to Nietzsche, are often exactly the opposite of what is avowed, even sincerely avowed, and most problematically, the real motives are hidden *because the agent hides them*. So "the denier [*der Entsager*]" is really not just an ascetic, he is also "an affirmer": "*ein Bejahender*" (GS, §27, 50-51). A man who is committed to humility and who takes himself to be acting humbly is really trying to manifest his view of himself as superior and deceives himself about why he is acting as he is. A man who takes himself to be motivated by generosity as the right thing to do and acts generously is actually motivated by a desire to make others dependent on him. Christian love is a "strategic" form of hatred (GM, §8). A "magnanimous person [*der Grossmüthige*]" is "a person with a most extreme thirst for vengeance [*ein Mensch des äussersten Rachedurstes*]" (GS, §49, 62). Kindness and pity can often be acts of contempt, ways of making the objects of one's attentions smaller, inferior; commitment to unconditional obligation, as in Kant, understood as autonomy, is actually a form of "refined servility [*feinere Servilität*]" (GM, §5, 33).

The general principle is stated clearly in *The Gay Science*: "*Unconscious virtues.*—All qualities of a person of which he is conscious—and especially those he supposes to be plain and visible to others also—are subject to laws of development entirely different from those qualities which are unknown or badly known to him, which conceal themselves by means of their subtlety even from the eye of a rather subtle observer and which know how to hide as if behind nothing at all" (§8, 35). The phrase "know how to hide as if behind nothing at all" brings out clearly the difficulties and the clear (and by now familiar) paradox that Nietzsche wants to focus on and investigate. For it would appear that the psychological phenomena that interest Nietzsche (and that interest many of his French psychologist models) cannot be accurately classified either as the determination of conscious thought and choice by nonconscious corporeal drives, or as the working of unconscious desires and impulses, at least on one interpretation of Freud's primary processes. (More on this in a moment, too.) As is especially clear when Nietzsche's rhetoric turns to a *condemnation* of the dishonesty and cowardice of those who avow commitment to Christian and secularized Christian or humanist value, the subjects in question in some sense must know what they are up to, even while they hide it from themselves, just to be subject to such critiques of their honesty ("*Redlichkeit*"). This is what makes the project of shaming them a possible one and therefore also gives some hope for "transvaluation."

In other words, Nietzsche is often explicit that the phenomena he is interested in are phenomena of self-deceit. He mentions a similar phenomenon when talking about the slave revolt. And it is as puzzling and paradoxical as self-deceit itself: that the revolt was directed against the masters but the slaves attacked them "in effigy" (*GM*, I, §10, 20). The similar puzzle here is also to understand *how* an attack on an effigy could possibly be psychologically satisfying. We do not in some mad moment imagine that the dummy being burned *is* the football coach. For example, in discussing the Eleatics and their attempt to turn their philosophy of supreme rational order into a philosophy of life: "In order to claim all this they had to deceive themselves about their own state: they had fictitiously to attribute to themselves impersonality and duration without change. . . . They closed their eyes to the fact that they, too, had arrived at their propositions in opposition to what was considered valid, or from a desire for tranquility or sole possession or sovereignty" (*GS*, §110, 111). What is important is the phrase "they closed *their* eyes [*sie hielten* sich *die Augen*]."

And, in discussing the French seventeenth-century debate about drama and the Aristotelian unities, he invents a term of art to explain what he means to highlight in this phenomenon as of psychological import, the "add-on liars [*Die Hinzu-Lügner*]": "One lied to oneself, inventing reasons for these laws, simply to avoid admitting that one had become used to them and would no longer have it any other way. . . . Here we have the great dishonesty of conservatives of all times—they are the add-on liars" (*GS*, §29, 51).

Throughout the books of his mature period—*Thus Spoke Zarathustra, On the Genealogy of Morals,* and *Beyond Good and Evil* especially—this psychological phenomenon is at the center of Nietzsche's concerns and is what he is mostly referring to when he insists that the traditional interpretive notions of the manifest and the hidden, or appearance and essence, are inadequate to capture the phenomenon. The mistake is identical to the one made in thinking that what is hidden in a literary text can simply be "extracted" and placed on view in a literal form, as if criticism had as its goal paraphrase.

The image that sums all this up is the one we have already encountered before, and it bears repeating here, the one mentioned at the end of the second-edition preface of *The Gay Science*:

> And as for our future, one will hardly find us again on the paths of those Egyptian youths who endanger temples by night, embrace statues, and want by all means to unveil, uncover, and put into a bright light whatever is kept concealed for good reasons. No, this bad taste, this will to truth, to "truth at any price," this youthful madness in the love of truth, have lost their charm for us; for that we are too experienced, too serious, too merry, too burned, too profound. We no longer believe that truth remains truth when the veils are withdrawn: we have lived too much to believe this. Today we consider it a matter of decency not to wish to see everything naked, or to be present at everything, or to understand and "know" everything. (*GS*, preface, 8)

As we have discussed, the suggestion Nietzsche is making in all these remarks is about the right (and of course wrong) way to understand what we might call the logic of essence and appearance, inner and outer, depth and surface, in the wide variety of *psychological* phenomena Nietzsche treats and not coincidentally in the problem of interpretation he poses about his own text. Simply put: we think of interpretation as a task because we understand meaning to be hidden or inside texts, and that will now be important for the psychological sense of hiddenness to which he is appealing in his account of self-deception. And Nietzsche is trying to suggest why he thinks there is something inappropriate about looking for such a hidden meaning or inner psychological state under these assumptions, even while the "old philologist" had to concede that interpretation is often also difficult and risky. (So in psychological terms, what we need to understand is how some motivation can direct behavior even if hidden, a task obviously dependent on some understanding of how first-personal avowals of one's own mindedness can be hidden at all, how such an avowal can be both sincere and false.)

That is, as is already obvious, the "Egyptian youths" passage does not just point to a textual or hermeneutical problem but is deeply connected to how Nietzsche want us to understand the relation between surface and depth in psychology, or in more familiar terms between inner and outer in psychological explanation, and is obviously connected to his famous claim in essay I, paragraph 13, of *On the Genealogy of Morals* that was the subject of the last chapter.

What is important to note in this context is that the direction Nietzsche is suggesting still retains a place for, let us say, the doubleness of consciousness and so the possibility of something hidden from an agent, or a motive denied, even if with some sort of sincerity. As we saw in the last chapter, it is extremely important that, as with the logic of the grave-robber image, Nietzsche does not say or imply that there *is* only the flash but that the lightning is inseparable from the flash. In the account of slave morality, for example, it is important that Nietzsche does not say that there simply are slavish types and slavish conduct, as if the outer expression of a certain hidden, inner drive. Slavish activity also has to be understood in a way by such subjects, taken to mean in a way, and such activity thus can either succeed or fail to embody the meaning that it is supposed to bear and cannot be understood simply as effects. What is effected cannot be identified as such by anything "behind" the deed. Slavish behavior is not the mere comportment of some bodily movements; it exists as such only in some sort of self-relation in relation to an other. In fact, what sort of bodily movement such conduct is is itself always a matter of contestation and uncertainty, a feature of it lost if it is crudely viewed as just the effect of a drive. The slavish also became divided against themselves; that is, they revolted, something both slavish and not slavish, a double consciousness. They can hide from themselves the cruelty in their morality of sympathy and pity, but if they are actually to be exercising cruelty, it must be "hidden in plain sight," or, as he says, "as if behind nothing at all." Likewise, I don't think there is much doubt that Nietzsche would want to distinguish between mere success at subduing another (as if "the expression of the will to power") and, say, nobility or even beauty in doing so, that nobility or beauty for him is different from mere success or thuggery, and that difference has to do with how something is done, with the state of mindedness involved. The *way* in which something is undertaken can also be false, however, a lie. But as with the famous paradox of self-deceit, whatever is hidden must be hidden in plain sight; otherwise, it would not be something one hides from oneself.

In the psychological case, interpretation is also not a matter of simply finding what lies hidden, as if looking for the cause of a symptom.

It matters that the conscious self-understanding is an attempted evasion of another and truer self-understanding, just as it matters that the latter is being hidden. We need to attend to both aspects to understand what is going on. It matters, that is, to the psychological meaning at issue, and the role of such self-ascriptions in the economy of agency cannot be separated out. So to add to the complexity of the picture Nietzsche is giving us, it is not only what is hidden that is relevant to the proper explanation and evaluation of action; we also have to consider just *how* what is hidden *is* hidden. That, too, tells us a great deal about what an agent is attempting. So in paragraph 44 in *The Gay Science*, "Important as it may be to know the motives from which humanity has acted so far, it might be more essential to know the belief people had in this or that motive, i.e. what humanity has imagined and told itself to be the real lever of its conduct so far. For people's inner happiness and misery has come to them depending on their belief in this or that motive—not through the actual motives" (*GS*, §44, 59).

IV.

Let me now return to the issues of why what Nietzsche is proposing cannot be understood as a causal determination by somatic forces "outside" the psychological, as I have put it.[1] Imagine a case in which it *would* be quite plausible to explain the psychological by appeal to the nonpsychological. Imagine a psychology laboratory experiment. (This is in fact an actual experiment, but I won't bother here with the footnote-necessary details, so let us treat it as imaginary. The point is the same.) A group of college students are told that they will be participating in a study about moral assessment. They watch videos of actors acting out moral violations ranging from the minor ("white lies") to the serious (stealing a laptop) to the egregious (a violent crime). They are given a scale and asked to evaluate the seriousness of the

---

1. I am trying here to meet a request for clarification about this issue raised by Jim Conant at an APA Author Meets Critics session on the French version of this book. (See Conant forthcoming.) The issue concerns what is actually meant by *prereflective*—whether it means somatic or in some way an aspect of active mindedness. I am trying to defend the latter, which I believe Conant was also suggesting.

infraction. Now imagine that one group of students are led into a viewing area that is terribly messy: old food wrappers and pizza boxes strewn everywhere, papers and notes scattered about, the floor sticky with spilled cola, and so forth. The other group is led into a pristine viewing room, sparkling clean and extremely orderly. The results of the experiment are that the students in the messy room are far more lenient in their judgments than the other group or various control groups in rooms different enough so that we can be sure that it is the messiness that is the influential factor.

I doubt that we would say that the lenient students unconsciously "wanted" to make their judgments cohere with the disorder of the environment, or unconsciously wanted to conform to what they assumed the messy-room-organizers must have wanted, or anything like that. *Wanting, intending,* or *trying* at whatever level of consciousness is not in the picture. Both their conscious evaluative standards and any unconscious reasons or motives they might have for having such standards—in this case, the whole domain of psychological candidates for explanation—do not seem relevant. They are not doing or trying to do anything. Something is *happening to them* that influences what they take to be decisions and is influencing that process from, as I am saying, the "outside." Some sort of cue is shifting or, one might say, interrupting and exogenously directing that decision process just as we might say if we discover that there is a drug that makes people much less morally judgmental.

I think that the passages we have already seen make clear that Nietzsche is not suggesting an "extrapsychological" drive theory but that he wants to be considered as offering a more complex psychological explanation—more complex than what the agent would consciously avow but still, to continue the image, "inside" the psychologically explicable. (You cannot *lie* to yourself, as in the "add-on liar" passage, without in some way knowing the truth; likewise with closing one's own eyes to something one *has seen and can see,* or deceiving oneself.) And this brings us to another possible model for such a complex psychology—the Freudian notion of the unconscious. And there do seem to be numerous similarities, many of them often noted, on issues such as "internalization," the pain and unpredictable consequences of repression and even sublimation. And we have many passages like the one we started with, in which Nietzsche speaks of such things as "unconscious covering." But the extent of the similarities depends on the interpretation of Freud.

That is, speaking very simply, there are also, paralleling the issue just discussed, two ways of sketching the Freudian notion of the unconscious. On one account, an appeal to the unconscious in an explanation of some human action is a dramatic *extension* of the domain of the psychological. Various pathological symptoms can certainly look as if someone is afflicted by an illness, in the way breathing might be impaired by an infection or one's ability to drive affected by alcohol. But Freud's genius, on this account, was to have been able to show that what appeared as symptoms I *suffered* could be understood as *psychologically motivated deeds* that I am trying to accomplish; they could be understood as actions, not mere natural events or sufferings. If I recoil in unreasonable horror from cats, am tormented by persistent thoughts that there may be some lurking about everywhere, and have no convincing explanation for such a phobia, I can be said to have some reason for such avoidance behavior, but in some way a reason not accessible by me. (Perhaps I am "trying to prove" that I do not have some weird desire to mate with felines, or I am trying to avoid various desires for my mother, whom I always associate with cats; whatever.) I have an unconscious reason or motive. My act remains psychologically explicable, but now the psychological has expanded to include unconscious motives and ends and desires.

On the other hand, we can think of the unconscious, the site of primary processes, as a kind of radically independent second mind, only this time the drives typical of such a material mind are more like a brute, nonintentional force intruding on and affecting and interfering with the conscious mind. I must be said, on this model, to have been seized by a material force; something has taken hold of me. I cannot be said to be attempting anything; there is no motivated irrationality. If I am visited by persistent intrusive thoughts, I am not attempting anything by *my* obsessively attending to such a content; something in the mental wiring has gone haywire; something is happening to me. (Many explanations of self-deception, of course, not just Freud's, rely on such a second-mind theory.) Whatever is responsible for altering and directing one's conscious moral assessments in our experiment example is to be compared with this second material mind, influencing and directing from "outside" the psychological.

Again, I think that the passages we have cited and many more that could be cited show that Nietzsche's account can be called Freudian but only if we claim that his language of instincts and drives and unconscious motives is much closer to the former, psychologically expansive Freud than to the two-mind, "suffering-from-material-forces" Freud. But if that is so, then before we proceed any further, we need to confront an obvious, perhaps fatal objection to any model of the mind, Nietzsche's or Freud's, that assumes self-deceit.

V.

The objection is a familiar one, often directed against appeals to self-deception, and is stated with typical bluntness by Rüdiger Bittner in an article entitled "Ressentiment." He poses a simple question for the canonical understanding of the slave revolt in morality. "It is hard to understand why people should in these circumstances produce a false story of that sort. They know that it is a mere story. After all, they make it up themselves."[2] Bittner concedes that the phenomenon that accounts like Nietzsche's assume is taken to be quite common, as in Jean de La Fontaine's famous fable of the fox who cannot leap high enough for some grapes and then, somehow, convinces himself that they were sour anyway. How could *that* be consoling, Bittner asks, given that the fox must know he is making up such a story as compensation for not being able to leap high enough? And "know" in such a criticism cannot be avoided if the phenomenon in question is to be understood, not evaded. That is, it begs the interesting question at issue to suggest that some desire or passion distorts belief formation, so influences that process that the fox attends only to evidence that preserves his pride and is moved to underplay evidence that wounds his pride, as in some accounts of the possibility of self-deception.[3] Again, something would then be happening in effect *to* the fox; the fox would not be intentionally deceiving himself. If the rejoinder to this insistence is

2. Bittner 1994, 130.

3. I think Poellner (2004) shows very well why the traditional analyses that try to defuse the paradoxical nature of self-deception do not work in Nietzsche's case.

simply to say that however difficult it is to explain, the phenomenon is so widespread in "ordinary humankind" that it *must* exist, the bullet-biting Bittner just notes that in that case "ordinary humankind begins to look pretty mad itself."[4] What we must do on his account is give up the notion that there is anything like self-deception, and so we must simply reject the very large number of passages in which Nietzsche relies on that model of the relation between appearance and essence, conscious and unconscious. Instead, Bittner encourages us to accept some version of a nonpsychological explicans prominent in our experiment example and in the materially minded Freud. "On the revised account [of the slave revolt] it is the same story—only the slaves didn't *do* it. Nor did anyone else. Madness just grew from suffering, and as it brings fresh suffering with it, what we have is just suffering proliferating. Metaphysical and moral notions did debase mankind, perhaps ruinously. But it is an illness, not a poisoning."[5] Bittner admits that "Nietzsche clearly rejects the proposed revision,"[6] but, he argues, so much the worse for Nietzsche. He should have relied more on his nonintentional model, his naturalism, visible in such claims from *Beyond Good and Evil* as "A thought comes when 'it' wants, not when 'I' want" (*BGE*, §17, 17).

But this all seems very hasty. Bittner is clearly operating with a strict and somewhat facile disjunction between simply knowing one's own mind (completely, transparently, and apparently unproblematically) and not knowing it. If one knows one's own mind, one apparently knows it fully; if one doesn't, then one simply and fully doesn't. On such assumptions, it is not surprising that self-deception or wishful thinking or sour grapes are all unintelligible. Of course, his claim will be that on *any* version of self-knowledge, the paradox of hiding something from yourself will return, but before writing off the bulk of what Nietzsche has to say about the issue, we should note what assumptions about self-knowledge are behind his account of such phenomena as the slave revolt in morality. That is what I propose to do now.

4. Ibid., 131.
5. Ibid., 134.
6. Ibid.

VI.

The question is what Nietzsche means by such remarks as "Everyone is farthest from himself" (*GS*, §335, 187). Does he mean, as he might, that we have not yet understood the prepsychological mechanisms that steer and direct behavior, behavior that we, in our ignorance, pretend that we are directing by conscious reflection and decisions; that is, that we simply have not understood the real motivations for which we pretend we understand? On this view, he would just be pointing out our ignorance, now gradually coming to an end. But in his *Genealogy*, he goes further, and it is clear that he means that we are not merely ignorant, but "we are unknown to ourselves," and this has a "good reason ... that we have never looked for ourselves" (*GM*, preface, 3). This claim—that we have "fled" from ourselves, to use the Sartrean language[7]—has the hint of what Nietzsche makes clearer in many places: that we have not simply by chance failed to seek ourselves. We are afraid and can be said to stand "far" from ourselves because we have essentially run away. But even at this level, this leaves much open. He could be claiming that we are unwilling to acknowledge how little we are in control of what we naively count as actions. Or does he mean to ask about what we might call "culpable" ignorance, in which we suspect something about ourselves that we do not pursue, in which we could know something crucial about ourselves but refuse, out of cowardice or laziness, simply to ask?[8] Or does he mean that we find ways to discount and even hide what we *do* know about ourselves? In all these latter senses, though, once we concede there is some measure of "hiding from ourselves," Bittner's skepticism becomes relevant again.

But if we take in a broad range of relevant passages, then despite the fact that we are so used to the notion that Nietzsche has some sort of drive theory or that he is offering a naturalistic account of human conduct based on some claim about a drive to gain and hold power, especially over others, we can at least see how far he is from such a

7. Poellner (2004) brings Sartre's analysis to bear on Nietzsche in quite an interesting way.

8. There is an element of this in Poellner's account. "The resolve not to engage in reflection in certain experiential contexts is itself an unthematic intention essential to the form of self-deception which *ressentiment* exemplifies" (2004, 62).

model of psychic dynamics. For one thing, he points out frequently that it is very unclear in one situation or another what counts as having achieved power, something not often stressed in "will to power drive" theories. It is this element of the interpretive play involved in self-avowals that greatly alters the standard picture of self-deception and suggests a different way to look at the phenomenon in question. Contrary to the sadistic, power-mad Nietzsche interpretations, "The state in which we hurt others is certainly seldom as agreeable, in an unadulterated way, as that in which we benefit others; it [having to hurt others] is a sign that we are still lacking power, or it betrays a frustration in the face of this poverty. . . . Only to the most irritable and covetous adherents of the feeling of power—to those for whom the sight of those who are already subjected (the objects of benevolence) is a burden and boredom—might it be more pleasurable to imprint the seal of power on the reluctant" (GS, §13, 39). "Strong" and "weak," he reminds us, "are relative concepts," and he often suggests that the truly powerful is he who need no longer have any interest in power as ordinarily understood, who is powerful enough to be indifferent to the question of power.

In many similar remarks, the central issue concerns the complexities of interpretation, interpreting the motives one ascribes to oneself and to others, and interpreting the meaning of the deed itself. And we are now in a position to make use of the results of the last chapter to suggest how Nietzsche understands the complexities of self-knowledge and how that bears on this issue. For, as we have seen, Nietzsche, like many other philosophers on this issue, from Wittgenstein to Elizabeth Anscombe to Sartre to Richard Moran to David Finkelstein, does not think self-knowledge is ever directly observational or introspectable. But what makes his position so unusual is that he *also* does not, by contrast, consider it immediate, self-presenting, or incorrigible. As we have seen, he wants to reject the model of individual agents whose subjective states cause bodily movement. The subject, he insists, is not "behind" the deed but "in" it. And, as we saw in the last chapter, this makes any claim for such self-knowledge necessarily provisional and contestable, realized or fully actualized only *in* the deed. This condition on any report of self-knowledge—that it is the result of provisional and testable interpretation, not inspection—will end up making the self-deceit problem somewhat more tractable.

It is of course true that Nietzsche often appeals to "instincts" or "drives" as if he were appealing to brute natural forces that operate outside of conscious control in any sense. But it is also extraordinary how far he goes in denying the immediacy of even any such supposedly immediate, self-presenting inner experience. He even says, "That a violent stimulus is experienced as pleasure or pain is a matter of the interpretive intellect, which, to be sure, generally works without our being conscious of it and one and the same stimulus can be interpreted as pleasure or pain" (*GS*, §127, 122). Or, in speaking about the origin of religion, "What led to the belief in 'anther world' in primordial times was not a drive or need, but an error in the interpretation of certain natural events, an embarrassing lapse of the intellect" (*GS*, §151, 131). Likewise, when describing much philosophy as an illness, Nietzsche does not think of such philosophy as simply a manifestation of a diseased body but as something much more complicated. "Philosophy has been no more than an interpretation of the body and a misunderstanding of the body. Behind the highest value judgments that have hitherto guided the history of thought are concealed misunderstandings of the physical constitution" (*GS*, preface, 5).

VII.

So the *paradox* of self-deception assumes something Nietzsche is skeptical about: the traditional paradox assumes that there are, on the one hand, to-be-inspected, real, determinate, and causally efficacious motives and intentions that really produce bodily actions, and, on the other hand, there are causally idle, fictional motives made up by a subject who pretends, against the facts (which he knows), that these fictional motives are the causally efficacious ones. Since the assumption is that the actual motives are psychological phenomena that can only be satisfied "inside" consciousness, they must *be* "inside" consciousness, or known as such by the subject, in which case we have the nearly insuperable difficulty: how could he pretend that he is motivated otherwise? Nietzsche is rejecting this whole model: the account of mindedness, self-knowledge, and action explanation that it involves. Everything, that is, depends on the proper attention to the way he treats the subject-deed relation in *On the Genealogy of*

Morals, essay I, paragraph 13, on his, I want to say, extreme insistence that *"Das Thun ist alles,"* the "deed is everything." In telegraphic form: self-knowledge is not observational but interpretive and, let us say, always promissory, futural, as complexly interpretive as the interpretive question of just what it is that is being done; action explanation is not causal, and motives cannot be understood as fixed, datable mental items. Rather, self-ascribing a motive is more like provisionally trying out an interpretation. On such a picture, it is not so paradoxical to suggest that the content of some avowal and the right act description are so pregnant with plausible possibilities that the prospect of self-serving or self-aggrandizing interpretations might not look so counterintuitive. Being aware of what is to oneself an unpleasant interpretive possibility about oneself and, under the press of its unpleasantness, manufacturing another roughly plausible interpretation is not like looking away from a causally effective determinate motive that is nevertheless paradoxically still "there," still before the mind's eye.

This raises the obvious question about what Nietzsche is willing to count as a correct or honest rather than self-serving interpretation (that is, if fidelity to a mental fact is not what he means). We cannot answer such a question without much more attention to what Nietzsche considers full practical self-knowledge, but we already have seen many important elements of that account. That evidence is that the realization that some self-serving interpretation is not true is not arrived at by some way of looking more deeply and accurately into a person's soul. If we think of any present avowal of motives as more like provisional commitments to act, based on various highly provisional and uncertain interpretations of one's personal history, past and present motives, and context, then the inaccuracy of some self-ascription is no great paradox and can be confirmed (if it can be) by what occurs *in the future*, is manifest in what, over time, the agent does and does not do (assuming again the same interpretive complexity about the meaning of future actions). In other words, the assumption that generates the problem Bittner is worried about is the assumption of a momentary or punctuated observation that a subject then tries to hide or flee from. So, to return to his example, it is far too crude to say simply that the rebelling slaves "knew they were making up a false story." What they took themselves to be doing is something considerably more open to interpretive finesse and is much more flexible and temporally extended than the description "They knew they were making it up" can allow.

This sort of account is consistent with many of the other things Nietzsche wants to say about human mindedness. To repeat a point made in chapter 3, in the *Genealogy*, he insists that some social and historical achievement is necessary before it would make sense to evaluate ourselves and others with the notions of "intentional," "negligent," "accidental," "accountable," and their opposites (*GM*, II, §4, 39–40). Such a mode of self-understanding is not to be understood as a claim for metaphysical truth but is itself an achieved interpretation in one community at a time of what could be and has been interpreted in many different ways. And it makes clearer why, in discussing the will to power, he says such things as, "Everything that occurs in the organic world consists of overpowering, dominating, and in their turn overpowering and dominating consist of re-interpretation, adjustment, in the process of which their former 'meaning' [*Sinn*] and 'purpose' must necessarily be obscured or completely obliterated" (*GM*, II, §12, 51).

Accordingly, when we read such ubiquitous remarks by Nietzsche as, in *Twilight of the Idols*,

> A person is necessary, a person is a piece of fate, a person belongs to the whole, a person only *is* in the context of the whole,—there is nothing that can judge, measure, compare, or condemn our being, because that would mean judging, measuring, comparing, and condemning the whole. . . . *But there is nothing outside the whole!*—The fact that nobody is held responsible anymore, that being is not the sort of thing that can be traced back to a *causa prima*, that the world is not unified as either a *sensorium* or a "spirit," *only this can constitute the great liberation,*—only this begins to restore the *innocence* of becoming. (*TI*, 182)

we have assembled the resources to provide an interpretation other than one that in effect denies there is any human agency at all, as if there were only the result of instinct causation; *or* as if one knew that one were acting on motives other than the one that one avows, but one somehow could hide that knowledge from oneself. Nietzsche could rather be insisting that the phenomena of self-serving interpretation and the self-inflating exaggeration of one's avowed commitments are extremely widespread and not paradoxical. The claim should be taken to mean one's *own professed interpretations* are always (or almost always) skewed, biased in ways that can take advantage of the many interpretive possibilities in human agency, all for the sake of some self-inflation. One finds a way to discount contrary evidence (of less noble motives, for example) in the same way that there are always pieces of textual evidence contrary to a proffered interpretation that one can find a way to discount. So, in practical knowledge, what bears out and so confirms some self-interpretation turns on such issues as consistency with what one actually does and how else one interprets one's own and others' motives.

Now this might seem just to reraise the paradoxical issues, but in another place. That is, how can one then go on to hide from oneself *the lack of fit over time between one's avowals and the pattern of one's actions* if that, what one actually does, is what provides the true content of one's actual motivation or real commitments? What I have said, suitably expanded and qualified and shown in more detail to be Nietzsche's actual view, might make it at least possible to say something on the face of it still highly contestable: that at the time of the slave revolt, in morality the question of "what actually motivated" the creation and application of new moral categories cannot be answered when put in this form, as if motives and intentions were datable, occurrent psychic forces (forces one could somehow become directly aware of and pretend not to be directly aware of). The manifest avowals of allegiance to values such as equality and humility as the basis for the condemnation of the masters *could have been "true."* What *makes* them untrue is not that they are made up at the time by slaves who pretend to be committed to them but who are really, at the time, knowingly seething with ressentiment, but that the future history of this moral institution betrays its true allegiances. Not for nothing does Nietzsche at the end of book I of *On the Genealogy of Morals* quote the original Tertullian about the pleasures of the saved in seeing the damned suffer.

So it would be simplistic in another way if one claimed to see obvious paradox in the evident inconsistency between one's avowals and one's deeds over time. Such a claim is also made in a domain of very wide interpretive possibility, and it is not hard to imagine the defenders of Christian morality able to rationalize away every piece of evidence for such an inconsistency brought up by Nietzsche or a

Nietzschean, including the Tertullian passage and the Christian fantasies in general about divine punishment.[9]

Finally, this is all quite consistent with a famous Nietzschean ideal, perhaps his most enthusiastically expressed, positive ideal that follows immediately from this way of understanding a possible gap between avowal and actual deed, between interpretation and its implications for action and other interpretations. As Nietzsche puts it, the Nietzschean "conscience" does not encourage us to admit who one is, or that one should be true to one's nature. This is not the right contrast or opposite to self-deceit. The achievement of true practical knowledge about oneself would be the successful fulfillment, in one's deeds, of the supreme Nietzschean imperative: *"Du sollst der werden, der Du bist."* *"Become* who you are!" (*GS*, §270, 152).

9. Interpretation, or rather strategic misinterpretation, also plays an interesting role in the account Poellner (2004) wants to ascribe to Nietzsche, but in a different way than that suggested here.

CHAPTER SIX

How to Overcome Oneself: On the Nietzschean Ideal

I.

Finally, how does Nietzsche's unusual position on agency, self-knowledge, value, and desire intersect with the most important and complicated modern philosophical issue? Given all that we have seen, does it matter to Nietzsche whether individuals are free in any of the manifold senses that have been so important throughout the philosophical tradition (self-knowledge, voluntarist "spontaneity," self-realization, autonomy, freedom from external constraint, morality, rational agency, authenticity, "nonalienated" identification with one's deeds, power)? And if persons are or can become in any of these senses or in any other sense free, *how* important is it to him that all or some or a small few should be able to attain such a state or to exercise such a capacity?

On the surface at least, even given the great variety of interpretations of Nietzsche and the variety of positions attributed to him, the problem of freedom, whether as a metaphysical issue or as a possible human aspiration in any of the above senses, does not seem to be one of his central concerns. He often gives the impression that he thinks discussions of such topics are pointless and are motivated in self-deceit. However, it would appear that there is a sense of freedom, one at least somewhat still connected to much of our intuitive and every-day understanding of freedom, that is quite important to Nietzsche. It is the topic he discusses under the label "self-overcoming." Or so I want to argue in this final chapter.

But to get to that issue, one should note first some of the details of his impatience with the "problem of free will" and with assessments of the "value of freedom," especially as those have been understood in Christian apologetics and in Western metaphysics from Augustine to Kant and Arthur Schopenhauer. Perhaps it would be better to say that his only interest in such questions is in dissolving the problems, not re-solving them, as we have already noted. In that much-cited discussion of the metaphysical issue of the *causa sui* in paragraph 21 of *Beyond Good and Evil*, he not only dismisses the voluntarist or incompatibilist commitment to such a *causa sui* (which he calls "a type of logical rape [*Notzucht*] and abomination [actually just *"Unnatur"* in the original]" [*BGE*, §21, 21]), but he goes on to be equally severe about what would appear to be its metaphysical contrary, the "unfree will" or the posi-tion of determinism. Both positions are said to be mere "mythologies"; and he encourages us to see that the real problem (the problem as it is manifested in "real life") is the distinction and contestation between "strong" and "weak" wills. Even this will not be easy to understand since in paragraph 19 of *Beyond Good and Evil*, Nietzsche had already effectively dismantled and rejected what would seem to be all the ele-ments necessary for claiming that there is any faculty of the will at all, distinct from thought and desire. He reinterprets what had been taken as "the will" as in reality a "complex of feeling and thinking" that can produce a distinct sort of affect and pleasure (in commanding). It is this affect that is mistakenly interpreted as "the will" (*BGE*, §19, 18–19; cf. *D*, 103).

In passages like these, we can at least see what *does* interest Nietzsche about this and all other traditional philosophical positions: an etiology and often a genealogy of the psychological type to whom one or the other of these positions would appeal. As in many other cases, here, too, philosophical positions are treated as psychological symptoms, and so an invitation to speculate on the need one type or another would have to believe either in a self-causing spontaneity or in what Nietzsche calls the "dominant mechanistic stupidity" of causal necessity. In this case he speculates on the stake a sort or type or "race"—"the vain race"—would have in taking absolute credit for their deeds, and the stake that those motivated by self-contempt and so an interest in "shifting the blame" from their contemptible selves would have. They (the determinists) disguise this "personal" need when they write books, Nietzsche says, and adopt "their most attractive disguise ... socialist pity" (*BGE*, §21, 22).

This same psychological inflection is apparent in his treatment of the political aspiration to achieve a free life, a life wherein one would be able to develop one's capacities and/or pursue one's preferences with minimal external constraint by others. In paragraph 260 of *Beyond Good and Evil*, at the end of his concise summary of the difference between master and slave morality, he applies this psychological typology and suggests that a desire for freedom from external constraint is typical of the slavish, while, by contrast, "artistry and enthusiasm in respect and devotion" characterize the noble type.[1]

II.

Let us say, then, that Nietzsche seems primarily interested in freedom as a value or an aspiration, has his own views about the nature of genuine freedom, and is especially interested in the psychology and psychological typology that would help explain genuine freedom (the "psychology of freedom," one might say), and the psychology behind differing understandings of freedom, what is at stake in the appeal of one or another aspiration, all presumably with the hope that we might eventually see which sorts of ideals and aspirations might be admirable and which not (although, again, the connection between diagnosis and evaluation, here as elsewhere in Nietzsche, is not obvious). Finally, whatever this psychological treatment is, it is neither an empirical psychology nor a philosophical psychology modeled after either Aristotle or Hume and, let us recall one last time, seems modeled after the older French sense of a *moraliste*.

---

1. Cf. *TSZ*, 46: "Free *from* what? What does Zarathustra care! But brightly your eyes should signal to me: free *for what*?"

Some aspects of what results from this approach to freedom are of course well known. If herd morality, conformism, and sheeplike timidity are to be held in contempt, then some contrary seems suggested, some ideal of *social independence* and a kind of *self-rule* or *self-reliance*. A Stoic-like emphasis on self-rule is particularly prominent in later works, *Twilight of the Idols* especially. There in paragraph 38 of the "Expeditions of an Untimely Man" section, called "My Conception of Freedom," Nietzsche offers an encomium to a wide-ranging set of psychological dimensions of freedom. "That one has the will to self-responsibility. That one preserves the distance that divides us. That one has become more indifferent to hardship, toil, privation, even to life. The man who has become free . . . spurns the contemptible sort of well-being dreamed of by shopkeepers, Christians, cows, women, Englishmen and other democrats. The free man is a warrior" (*TI*, 213–14).

The passage goes on like this, praising danger, risk, and strength, but, as he tries to characterize what he calls "psychologically true [*psychologisch wahr*]" about freedom, Nietzsche adds something that is easy to overlook. "How is freedom measured, in individuals as in nations? By the resistance which has to be overcome, by the effort it costs to stay aloft. One would have to seek the highest type of free man where the greatest resistance is *constantly being overcome*" (ibid.; my emphasis).

Nietzsche here is most interested in a sort of psychological self-relation as constitutive of freedom (a self-relation that would immediately define of itself acceptable and unacceptable relations to others), and he clearly thinks of this psychological state as an achievement along a spectrum of possibilities, not an either-one-has-it-or-one-doesn't kind of capacity, as among the voluntarists, an achievement that he also treats in a sort of soul-writ-large way, ascribing this achievable state to possible nations as well.[2] And he notes that whatever the resistance that has to be overcome, there results no settled state; the

2. On this account, freedom for Nietzsche involves achieving a certain sort of relation to oneself that only a few are capable of, and, it would appear, that cannot be the product of any sort of direct intention by an individual. The conditions for its achievement depend on far more than individual "willpower." This means such a notion of freedom does not rely at all on a libertarian or "could have unconditionally done otherwise" conception of freedom. See the valuable discussion by Ken Gemes (2006), especially his case for this "achievement" sense of freedom and Nietzsche's compatibilism.

resistance must be constantly (*beständig*) overcome (*überwunden*). (He notes that he understands freedom as the Romans and Venetians did, as "something you have and do not have, as something that you will, that you win" [*TI*, 214].) Earlier in *Twilight*, in paragraph 3 of "Morality as Anti-nature," he had both stressed this notion of achievement and also characterized it as an odd sort of calm amid unsettled endeavors. "Or the expression of ripeness and mastery in the middle of doing, making, effecting, willing and a tranquil breathing, an attained 'freedom of the will' [*die erreichte Freiheit des Willens*]. . . . Twilight of the Idols [*Götzendämmerung*]: who knows? Perhaps this is just a type of 'peace, fullness of soul' [*Frieden der Seele*]" (*TI*, 174).

III.

But what *is* this sort of self-relation? What counts as self-mastery in this sense? Two elements have been suggested in recent discussions. One is inspired by passages in *The Gay Science*, echoed elsewhere, about what appears to be a kind of literary self-creation as the "greatest will to power," the desire "to impose upon becoming the character of being" (*WP*, 330). On this view, freedom for Nietzsche has elements both of a self-realization theory ("how to become *what* you are," the subtitle of *Ecce Homo*—i.e., become, own up to being, the kind of creature who must fashion his own character and personality) and an authenticity theory (as in passages in *Schopenhauer as Educator* and *The Gay Science* that insist that one ought to become who one individually is—"Be who you are" [*SE*, 127] in the former and "You should become who you are" [*GS*, §270, 152] in the latter). And according to these interpretations, these injunctions can be fulfilled if one creates oneself as if a "literary character" in a novel, "gives style" to one's character, finds a way to identify oneself with all one's actions, to see that no aspect of one's character and deeds can be what it is without literally every other aspect of one's character and deeds. This would be one way of attaining what appears to be the second necessary aspect of "*erreichte Freiheit* [achieved freedom]," a complete and hierarchical *unity* among states of one's soul, memories, desires, aversions, and so forth. We would thus have fulfilled what appears to be the ideal suggested by *The Gay Science*, paragraph 299, to become "the poets of our own lives," or the call to "become those who we are" in *The Gay Science*, paragraph 335, human beings who, Nietzsche says, "create themselves." We would not be what circumstances or others have made us, not be pulled or pushed about by whatever inclination or aversion we happen to be feeling, would be who we really, ontologically and individually, are, self-creating and individually self-created, hierarchically unified beings, and in that sense would have "reached" freedom.

There are several problems with this approach. In the first place, the formulation attributes to us a distinct power or capacity that seems to cry out for a further, deeper metaphysical account, something, I have suggested, inconsistent with Nietzsche's claim about the priority of psychology and too traditional to match his intentions. Why are we entitled to believe that we *can* assume such a possible independence between a creator or ruler self and a created object and "commonwealth"?[3] It seems just as implausible that one could assume such a detached, artistlike creator position as that, for any deed, one could have done otherwise.

Second, some aspects of the position seem wildly implausible. *Why* is it a condition of this literary unity that I must be able to understand *every* single deed of mine as necessary for another? That my getting a divorce or resigning my professorship is to be somehow understood as linked together with which tie I choose to wear or what I had for breakfast?

Third, the self-creation view often imports a notion of what *creation* is that is foreign to Nietzsche, whose sympathies here are not with the hypermodernist, ironic, insubstantial position of Rameau's nephew or Marcel Proust but remain essentially romantic. From the beginning of his publishing career to near the end, the creative state is always understood as Dionysean, a dissolution of boundaries and not their Apollonian establishment, a state of reverie and intoxication (*Rausch*).[4] In the *Zarathustra* chapter of *Ecce Homo*, he goes to great lengths to

3. Cf. *BGE*, §225, 117: "In human beings creature and creator are combined."
4. See *TI*, 195–96. Nietzsche can speak out of both sides of his mouth on this, praising *both* irony and wholeheartedness. Cf. *BGE*, §40, §284, §289, and contrast *TI*, 217–18. As we shall see, the tension created by such passages is not an oversight by Nietzsche. He very deliberately wants to claim both aspects as essential in "the achievement of freedom."

describe precisely the involuntariness and necessity of this creative state, insisting that he, as author, has virtually *vanished* (*EH*, 126–27), and his account of artists in *Beyond Good and Evil*, those for whom necessity and "freedom of the will" (cited with the usual sneer quotes by Nietzsche) are the same, makes the identical point even more clearly (*BGE*, §213). Even in the self-creation passage (§335) of *The Gay Science*, Nietzsche goes on to say that such creation requires that we learn "everything that is lawful and necessary in the world," that to become creators we have "to become physicists" (*GS*, §335, 189). (In the discussion of the "way of the creator" in *Thus Spoke Zarathustra*, Nietzsche's account does not sound like aesthetic self-creation: "With my tears go into your isolation, my brother. I love him who wants to create over and beyond himself and thus perishes" [*TSZ*, 48].)

Finally, and most important, the concept of creating oneself as if the author of one's life is inherently unstable, potentially incoherent. In literary terms, the character creating the unity of character in the story of one's life is obviously also a character himself *in* the story he is narrating. For *that* character to form a unity with the character being created, one will always require, in an obvious iteration, another creator-character who could bring the creator and created characters together, and so on. There are literary attempts to write the story of a character who finally becomes the author of the story of this becoming that we have just read. Proust is the obvious example. But the mere existence of that novel simply raises its own version of this problem, a legendary one for readers: how to understand the relation between the Marcel who is the object of the story, the older Marcel who appears to be narrating and writing the story, and the absent Ur-narrator, Proust himself. If anything, the briefest contemplation of the details of this issue in Proust make much more unlikely the possibility of construing freedom as the self-creation of a unified character.[5] And all of this is not yet to mention that this account leaves unclear how we are to put together the idea of an author/creator of one's own character with the requirement of some wholehearted identification with one's creation, something far more passionate and unqualified than any picture of a Rameau-like independence.

5. Cf. the compelling account of the relation between the younger Marcel, the older author-Marcel, and Proust the historical author in Landy 2004.

IV.

We move in a more promising direction, I want now to suggest, if we pay attention to another dimension central to Nietzsche's picture of agency, something already alluded to in several passages cited above. That is the fact that for Nietzsche one does not count as an *agent*, the true subject of one's deeds, just by in effect "showing up." One has to achieve something—and I am suggesting that this is a distinct sort of psychological self-relation, both attitudinal and dispositional—in order to be capable of any real practical intentionality or real agency. (I say here "one has to achieve," but, as we shall see shortly, it is important to note that there is no reason to think that Nietzsche must mean an exclusively individual achievement, the result of an individual's "resolve" and efforts. It could be, perhaps exclusively, a civilizational or social achievement, or even an achievement of fate that is responsible for one's being in such a self-relational state.) The state is described in any number of ways, but all of them have something to do with a kind of self-dissatisfaction, a generally negative as well as positive stance toward some current set of standing attitudes, commitments, and ideals. By and large, Nietzsche describes this condition when he wants to talk about, as he calls it, freedom of the *highest* sort, the *true* or paradigmatic instance of independence from others and a kind of self-direction, not humdrum or ordinary cases of such intentionality, like pumping water, or turning on the light switch, and so forth. All action involves a negation of a sort, an alteration of what would have remained the same without one's intervention, but Nietzsche appears particularly interested in a kind of inward-looking self-negation, a transformation of what had been a subject's restraints, or commitments, basic desires or passions, all in a way that makes possible a new kind of outward-looking relation to the world. In those paradigmatic cases (where, especially, the direction and course of one's whole life are at stake), he often focuses our attention on what he calls a "tension of the spirit" that allows a genuine "self-overcoming."[6]

One initial, still quite crude, summary of what Nietzsche is getting at in these passages would simply be that achieved freedom involves

---

6. These remarks are the beginnings of a response to questions about self-dissatisfaction and asceticism raised by Anderson (forthcoming).

achieving a capacity both to sustain a wholehearted commitment to
an ideal (an ideal that is worth sacrificing for, that provides the basis
for a certain hierarchical unity among one's interests and passions)
and what appears at first glance to be a capacity in some tension
with such wholeheartedness—a willingness to overcome or abandon
such a commitment in altered circumstances or as a result of some
development. To be unable to endure the irresolvable dynamic of
what Nietzsche calls an ideal's or a goal's or a value's constant self-
overcoming, to remain dogmatically attached to an already overcome
form of life (as with the Christians described in *The Anti-Christ* who,
as a result of the "self-overcoming of the intellect," know that prior
terms of belief can no longer be invoked in the same way but do so
anyway: "Everyone knows this: *and yet everything goes on as before*"
[*AC*, 34]), or to concede such mutability but with a cynical relativism
that prohibits any wholehearted identification with a new ideal (as
the "last men," such as those who so casually respond to the "God is
dead" news in paragraph 125 of *The Gay Science*), or to slide into a com-
placent, lazy identification with whatever is conventionally valued (as
Nietzsche says in the second *Untimely Meditation* of the Germans of
his own day, who have let themselves go and "elect for ease and com-
fort and the smallest possible degree of self-discipline" [*UM*, 80])—all
these are treated as forms of unfreedom.

To be sure, *freedom* is not the term Nietzsche prefers, although, as
we have seen, despite its dangerous associations, it is one he uses.[7]
He more often speaks of satisfying the conditions of life, leading a
life, truly living, recognizing one's life as one's own. The Nietzschean
"theory of agency" is couched in the elusive formulations we have
seen several times, as in "I wish your self were in the deed like the
mother is in the child; let that be *your* word on virtue," from *Thus
Spoke Zarathustra* (74). But the agency issues seem to me clearly present. This is so even though neither Nietzsche nor Zarathustra ever
simply encourages us to "overcome yourselves." (The issue seems to
be the proper acknowledgment and endurance of the self-overcoming

7. The well-known discussion of the "sovereign individual" in the second essay
of *GM* (II, §2) is another case in point, as is Nietzsche's discussion of the "right" to
make promises (*GM*, II, §1). Cf. the discussion of the general issue raised by such
claims in chapter 2 of this book.

character of life, an orientation that itself, as we shall see, has several social and historical conditions for its possibility.)

The achieved state of mind that Nietzsche promotes in these passages is not easy to make out. In the first place, underlying it appears to be a much broader theory about the historical fragility of all human norms, the inevitability not just of a kind of organic growth and death but of a self-undermining process that sometimes sounds positively Hegelian. It is this historical fate for norms that *requires* the kind of acknowledgment and endurance that Nietzsche praises when he discusses self-overcoming. Indeed, some of the references translated as "self-overcoming" are actually to the famously Hegelian term of art *"Selbstaufhebung"* and its cognates, as in *On the Genealogy of Morals* when Nietzsche claims that "every good thing on earth" eventually overcomes ["sublates"] itself, or later in *On the Genealogy of Morals* when Nietzsche proclaims what he calls the "law of life," "the law of the necessity of self-overcoming in the nature of life," where he uses both *Selbstaufhebung* and *Selbstüberwindung*. Morality's commitment to an ethic of truthfulness about intentions is his chief example of this self-undermining and self-overcoming, but as stated, it is presented as simply a law of life itself. (The death of Attic tragedy, which Nietzsche calls a suicide, a *Selbstmord*, might be another example of this law. So might truthfulness about the value of truth.)[8]

Second, the state itself, the proper responsiveness to the self-overcoming character of life, is quite complicated, full of dialectical, affirmation/negation flourishes, all of which evoke Nietzsche's characterization of freedom in *Twilight of the Idols*, that it is something one "has and has not." When Zarathustra discusses the "way of the lover," he characterizes it as "you love yourself and that is why you despise

8. In Hegel there is an elaborate speculative theory about why commitment to a certain norm or to any principle would, in the process of becoming a more articulated or self-conscious commitment, render continued allegiance more and more problematic until the original position was "negated" even while preserved and "raised up," or *aufgehoben*. There is no such theory in Nietzsche, although there are indications that he thinks that commitments require a certain sort of selective attentiveness, perhaps even a sort of self-delusion that is inevitably rendered more difficult with time. Cf. his summary of this "process" in *EH*: "The self-overcoming of morality, from out of truthfulness; the self-overcoming of moralists into their opposite—into me—that is what the name Zarathustra means coming from my mouth" (*EH*, 145).

yourself, as only lovers despise.... What does he know of love who does not have to despise precisely what he loved!" (*TSZ*, 48). As in *Human, All Too Human*, Nietzsche will frequently pronounce himself in favor of a morality "as a continual self-command and self-overcoming practiced in great things and in smallest" (*HAH*, 322), but his more detailed accounts of such a self-relational, self-overcoming state are even more figurative and more difficult to summarize. A typical passage is from his account of *Thus Spoke Zarathustra* in *Ecce Homo*: "The psychological problem apparent in the Zarathustra type is how someone who says no and *does* no to an unheard of degree, to everything everyone has said yes to so far,—how somebody like this can nevertheless be the opposite of a no-saying spirit ... how someone with the hardest, most terrible insight into reality, that has thought the 'most abysmal thought,' can nevertheless see it not as an objection to existence, not even to its eternal return,—but instead find one more reason in it for himself to be the eternal yes to all things" (*EH*, 130–31).

The language of a negation that is also an affirmation is sometimes transposed into a more familiar Nietzschean trope and one more familiar in compatibilist accounts of freedom, the simultaneity, in the experience of true freedom, of both freedom (the capacity to negate, free oneself from, some state or other) and necessity (the affirmation of a cycle of necessity). In the "Richard Wagner in Bayreuth" section of *Untimely Meditations*, Nietzsche claims that in listening to Wagner, one does not have the usual aesthetic experiences of enjoyment or interest:

> one feels only the *necessity* of it all. What severity and uniformity of purpose he imposed upon his will, what self-overcoming the artist had need of in the years of his development so as at last in his maturity to do with joyful freedom what was necessary at every moment of creation, no one will ever be able to calculate: it is enough if we sense in individual cases how, with a certain cruelty of decision, his music subordinates itself to the course of the drama, which is as inexorable as fate, while the fiery soul of this art thirsts to roam about for once unchecked in the freedom of the wilderness. (*UM*, 244)[9]

9. It is interesting that, when describing his own most difficult "self-overcoming," his break with Wagner, Nietzsche describes it both as a difficult act of self-overcoming but also as his fate, *Schicksal* (*CW*, 233).

The two sorts of formulations, necessity and freedom, affirmation and negation, are brought together in a still highly figurative passage in *The Gay Science*, paragraph 276.

> I, too, want to say what I wish from myself today and what thought first crossed my heart this year—what thought shall be the reason, warrant and sweetness of the rest of my life! I want to learn more and more to see what is necessary in things as what is beautiful in them—thus I will be one of those who make things beautiful. *Amor fati*: Let that be my love from now on! I do not want to wage war against ugliness. I do not want to accuse; I do not even want to accuse the accusers. Let *looking away* be my only negation! And, all in all and on the whole: some day I want only to be a Yes-sayer! (*GS*, §276, 157)

Finally, there is a last set of images that Nietzsche appears to treat as a condition for such a self-overcoming—that is, self-negating and yet self-identifying and self-affirming—state. These images continue the unusual emphasis of the passage just cited, where the achievement of freedom seems much more the achievement of an intellectual (i.e., "to learn more and more") and erotic (as in the references to his heart and what he hopes for his "love") attitude. This is consistent with the intellectualist account of freedom in Socraticism, Stoicism, and Spinoza, a notion for which Nietzsche expressed admiration. For Nietzsche, too, there *is* a kind of knowledge that will set one free, but it is not knowledge of the human good and not, or at least not wholly, the Spinozist knowledge of necessity. It appears to be a psychological realization of the ineliminable need for self-overcoming. The image is also consistent with the fact that, despite what can seem the hortatory character of Nietzsche's rhetoric, many of the passages we have looked at do not really directly encourage readers to *do* anything, as if simply to resolve to become free, to attain freedom. One cannot, as an act of will traditionally understood, will oneself into a state of knowledge or to desire something. The conditions for the attainment of freedom—the proper relation of attachment and detachment—seem, as they have several times before, largely prevoluntary and extend in scope beyond what individuals can do. Likewise, while Nietzsche is not encouraging anyone to "overcome himself," but rather writes about bearing or enduring a fate in a certain way, he is *also* still not encouraging one not to flee that fate, as if that, too, were a matter of simple resolve, but describing what it would be like for that fate to be borne or endured and affirmed, what else would have to be in place for that to happen, and what it would be like.[10] Thus the following images that suggest these necessary conditions.

There is a kind of culmination of this sort of language in the section "On Self-Overcoming" in *Thus Spoke Zarathustra*. In this section we hear again many of the themes sounded about self-overcoming. "Life" reveals to Zarathustra its "secret"—"I am that which must always overcome itself" (*TSZ*, 89). Any good and evil presumed not transitory are said "not to exist." "Driven on by themselves, they must overcome themselves again and again" (*TSZ*, 90). But now something else, apparently momentous, is added. We also learn that it is *this* feature of life—and Nietzsche seems to mean here this feature of the historical life of values, the feature of having to overcome itself—that is somehow equivalent to the claim that "all life is will to power."[11]

We have heard this link before, as in the *Human, All Too Human* remark about "continual self-*command and* self-*overcoming* practiced in great things and in smallest." But the conjunction of topics is puzzling. One set of images deals with the necessity of mastery and servitude in existence, the omnipresence of commanders and obeyers. The second deals with images of the transitoriness of any fixed, settled value and suggests the great difficulty of acknowledging, accepting, or "living out" in some way this perpetually self-undermining dynamic. Both,

10. This dimension obviously has many resonances in the Heidegger of *Being and Time*. Two are the clearest: Heidegger's description of authenticity as a "readiness" for anxiety, and so the stance of "anticipatory resoluteness" for a being that is always "ahead of itself"; and the fact that Heidegger does not think of the forgetfulness of the everyday as a "failure" of Dasein that we should be encouraged to avoid. Rather, such forgetfulness is as constitutive of what it is to be Dasein as authenticity. There is something of this in Nietzsche's discussion of the "clouds of illusion" necessary for the creation and affirmation in life.

11. I discuss the place and function of this ideal in *TSZ* as a whole in my "Introduction" to *TSZ* (Pippin 2006). Yet again all the important points in this treatment of the will to power are made figuratively, in this case in terms of the image of a "river" and "life" (see xxvff). Although I disagree with the intentionalist way in which Bernard Reginster puts the problem of self-overcoming (as if we are actually to create our own obstacles), there is much of value in his treatment of this theme and its relation to the will to power. See Reginster 2006 and my review, Pippin 2008b.

this unavoidable struggle for mastery and this ability to acknowledge the transitoriness of that in the name of which one claims mastery, seem related to Nietzsche's view of freedom.

The link between the will to power and self-overcoming appears to be related to the unusual way Nietzsche understands power or, more precisely, what he is willing to count as the realization of any will to power. For we recall that Nietzsche sometimes concedes that the most essential element in a contestation over power has to be the interpretive question of what *counts* as having achieved mastery. ("Everything that occurs in the organic world consists of overpowering, dominating, and in their turn overpowering and dominating consist of re-interpretation, adjustment, in the process of which their former 'meaning' [*Sinn*] and 'purpose' must necessarily be obscured or completely obliterated" [*GM*, II, §12, 51].) The ability to bully and tyrannize someone into cooperation is one thing, the ability to inspire true service is another; self-command is one thing, self-overcoming is another; being unimpeded in the satisfaction of one's desires is one thing, being able to order one's desires in a "hierarchy of rank" is another; commanding is one thing, being "strong" enough to "yield" command is another.

"*Yield* [*hingeben*]" is Nietzsche's word in the passage that links the themes of mastery and self-overcoming. "And as the smaller yields to the greater that it may have pleasure and power over the smallest, thus even the greatest still yields, and for the sake of power risks life. That is the yielding [*Hingebung*] of the greatest; it is hazard and danger and casting dice for death" (*TSZ*, 89, T).

The upshot of these obscure allusions seems to be that *nothing* really counts in some probative way as "*the*" establishment of mastery. There are, of course, wider, more apparently metaphysical dimensions of the will-to-power notion in Nietzsche's work, but in the most intuitively obvious instance—dominating and being dominated in the human sphere—these passages suggest that it is a mistake to understand the meaning of mastery in such a human dimension without taking into account the unsettled and precarious interpretation of mastery upon which the claim of having-mastered will always actually rest. These "interpretations" are mutable, of a time and place, and so true masters must be prepared to "yield" as well as to seize command. To be capable of this is to have achieved freedom; to become, in Nietzsche's earlier invocation of freedom, a *freier Geist*, a free spirit.[12] And all of this is apparently connected with the uniquely historical situation in which Nietzsche believes we must evaluate and act, the first epoch in which we must admit that we do not know, in the traditional objectivist or religious sense, what is worth wanting or aspiring to, where the danger of "nihilism" (on this reading, not a failure of knowledge or of will, but of desire) is always threatening. The prospect of a constantly "self-overcoming" structure of valuation is what obviously provokes this danger, and Nietzsche's aspiration is that such an age might also allow human beings who are prepared to be *constantly* "over" or beyond themselves—"*Übermenschen*," they might be called. He sums up such a stance in just this way in paragraph 347 of *The Gay Science*: "Conversely, one could conceive of such a delight and power of self-determination, a *freedom* of the will in which the spirit takes leave of all faith and every wish for certainty, practiced as it is in maintaining itself on light ropes and possibilities and dancing even beside abysses. Such a spirit would be the *free spirit* par excellence" (*GS*, §347, 206).

This is a tangle of themes, any one of which would require much more discussion. I have suggested that we should follow Nietzsche's lead in considering the "problem of freedom" to be a "psychological" problem in his sense of the term. That is, Nietzsche clearly considers freedom to consist in some sort of affirmative psychological relation to one's own deeds, a relation of identification, finding oneself in one's deeds, experiencing them as genuinely one's own. He also considers this state of being an achievement rather than the exercise of an inherent capacity. The achieved state in question requires an unusual intentional self-relation, in particular an intentional relation to one's own commitments. The relation involves both a kind of wholehearted identification and affirmation as well as the potential for great self-dissatisfaction. It is a state of extreme "tension." One is neither as passionately identified with one's projects as Goethe's Werther nor as

---

12. Cf. the discussion in II, §10, of *GM*, in which, in his genealogy of punishment, Nietzsche notes that "as a community grows in power, it ceases to take the offence of the individual quite so seriously," and that in the development of justice, it all "ends by turning a blind eye and letting off those unable to pay—it ends like every good thing on earth by sublimating itself" (47–48). ("Sublimate" is a strong translation for "*sich selbst aufhebend*." "By overcoming itself" would be a more natural translation.)

ironically detached from them as Denis Diderot's Rameau's nephew.
To be in such a state of tension is to be capable of self-overcoming,
genuine freedom, or, one might better say, to be capable of bearing the
burden of such self-overcoming and of affirming under its condition.
Yet the conditions for the possibility of such an achievement extend
far beyond what an individual alone can be called on to achieve. These
conditions are partly social and historical, and Nietzsche's basic psychology does not appear to include an addressee for any call to simple
resolve or strength of will. (Even if it did, a will cannot resolve to be
strong unless it already is.) Whatever the nature of the perspective
achieved by Montaigne that Nietzsche so much admired, it was not
achieved (cannot be achieved) by force of will or as the consequence of
practical reasoning. All of this is in partial explanation of Nietzsche's
unusual rhetoric, a mixture of so many different styles, tropes, and
voices, as he tries, in effect, to create a picture that can get some grip or
hold on his readers. This is especially true of Zarathustra, who, readers inclined to the bloodthirsty-blond-beast Nietzsche rarely notice,
is quite an unusual hero: often perplexed, confused, disappointed in
his comrades and followers, at times bombastic and self-important,
at times tender-hearted and resigned to his fate—a figure as much of
parody as of tragedy, a fact and paradox Nietzsche was himself eager
to point out. All of which raises the question that, in Nietzsche's terms,
arises within the perspective of "life"—what would it be both to live
out bearing the burden of the finitude and temporal fragility of one's
ideals and yet to be capable of "self-overcoming"?

These questions can be pursued in any number of ways. My point
here has only been to suggest that if the topic is freedom and self-rule
according to Nietzsche, any investigation of that issue will have to lead
to yet another unusual paradox in Nietzsche's account. There is, in
other words, an analogue here to the famous Pensée of Pascal's that
Nietzsche must have relished: "*Se moquer de la philosophie, c'est vrai-
ment philosopher.*" True philosophy ridicules, has nothing to do with,
"philosophy." The surprising Nietzschean turn of that screw would be
that the true realization of the will to power has nothing to do with
gaining and holding power as traditionally understood, except as an
indifference to power in this sense. The implication from the passages
we have reviewed would seem to be that the true realization of the
will to power, genuine freedom, has rather to do with self-overcoming.

Concluding Remarks

For all his aspirations and admiration, Nietzsche never succeeded in writing with the kind of "cheerfulness," "*Heiterkeit*," and balance of Montaigne. For one thing, in his eagerness to explore what the absence of any reliance on philosophical theory might amount to, he is led into such topics as those just discussed in the previous chapters. Exploring what *not relying* on the idea of a causally independent, persistent subject, supposedly transparent to itself, the "owner" of its intentions and thoughts, might amount to turns out to be a kind of mirror image of philosophical theory, antitheory conducted in images, metaphors, and similes, but in a certain sense trapped by the systematic ambition of what it is countering. Nietzsche clearly never resolved this difficult rhetorical problem. (Put another way, Montaigne did not have "Montaigne" as a standard or model the way Nietzsche did. Nietzsche's calls for a "kind of second innocence" make clear he is aware of this problem, but that does not mean he ever resolved it.)

For another thing, the shape of the emerging bourgeois world is much clearer and much more threatening three hundred years later and in Nietzsche's case provoked a much more violent, sometimes reckless response than anything one can find in Montaigne. This hostility of Nietzsche to what, in the interpretation presented here, we might call the "erotic timidity" of the late modern, bourgeois world—the world where health, security, prudence, and as long, comfortable, and happy a life as possible are the chief desiderata—is important not only because of the barrier it creates to any Montaigne-like state of psychic health and reconciliation and because of the unique way he poses the issues, but also because it was at once so influential and so representative, even in its uniqueness.

For, at just the moment in the nineteenth century when western European societies, for all of their massive faults, seemed to start paying off the Enlightenment's promissory notes—reducing human misery by the application of its new science and technology, increasing the authority of appeals to reason in public life, reducing the divisive public role of religion, extending the revolutionary claim of individual natural rights to an ever-wider class of subjects, accelerating the extension of natural scientific explanation, and more and more actually gaining what Descartes so prophetically promised, the mastery of nature—it also seemed that many of the best, most creative minds produced within and as products of such societies rose up in protest, even despair, at the social organization and norms that also made all of this possible.

No one, with the possible exception of Heidegger, is more important to and representative of this modernist mood, or "*Stimmung*," than Nietzsche. Somehow the "realizations" of freedom that had counted so heavily for the preeminent bourgeois philosopher, Hegel, had within the space of sixty years come to count for a great deal less, "psychologically," in the sense used here. It was Hegel who mounted the most ambitious case for the rationality of modern forms of ethical life and who insisted most emphatically that that rationality was not an abstract ideal, imperfectly but ever more successfully achieved, but that such rationality had, to use the Nietzschean word, a "life" in the historically actual social practices of giving and demanding justifications from each other. Hegel, that is, believed that the rule of law, basic rights protection, especially property rights, a market economy and a representative state, the satisfactions of romantic love and the modern or nuclear family, the protection of a zone of genuine privacy and real individuality, were all, in effect, *satisfaction enough*. That is, the transparency, rationality, and psychologically reconciling character of this institutional and private life were supposed to provide satisfaction enough.

Hegel was, understood historically, wrong ("psychologically wrong," let us say), and a good deal of later European high culture has to do with in just *what* sense he was wrong. The psychological sense suggested by Nietzsche is clear enough by now. This sort of a world, Hegel's world, both disguises from itself, in massive strategies of self-deceit, its own hidden brutality (think, for example, of the films of Claude Chabrol) and must end in an erotic failure, boring. It is as if the character in Hegel's great novel *Geist* had become a character in Proust's great novel, its erotic life threatened by or eventually destroyed by the crushing forces of habit, familiarity, banality, and repetition that Proust's characters struggle, neurotically and obsessively, to avoid with their jealous fantasies of secret lives and untrustworthy friendships. In other words, Nietzsche's implicit case to himself seems to be: you try putting Montaigne in the world of late-nineteenth- and early-twentieth-century Europe, *my* world, and you will not find such a sanguine, wise, cheerful observer.

But this leaves two open questions. One is a better understanding of just what *sort* of problem this "psychohistorical" assessment of erotic possibility amounts to. What does it mean to point out that Hegel was in effect wrong about whether this sort of "bow" would have enough "tension" to make possible some life-sustaining striving? The second is whether Nietzsche would be right about the *greater* burden of our "intellectual conscience" and the greater erotic failure of late modern, secular, humanist, liberal democratic Europe. Does the latter really explain the huge difference in tone between Nietzsche and Montaigne, the anxiety, anger, and what Nietzsche calls Zarathustra's "sickness with man himself"? Or would it be more correct to say that Montaigne has found a way of addressing what we now call the everyday, the quotidian, the common, without the expectations of religious transcendence, military glory, martial virtues, and philosophical notions of perfection and perfectibility, while still being receptive to small-scale moments of grace and even a kind of redemption? Does this historical difference explain the fact that Nietzsche is still trapped in and is still burdened by such hierarchical aspirations, that by contrast Montaigne has found "enough" worthy of love strictly from the perspective of the "human, all too human," and that the clearest sign that Nietzsche has not, that something is going wrong, misfiring, is that he *still* measures what he sees from a perspective that would have puzzled his hero,

Montaigne, the perspective of eternity (the eternal return of the same) and the perspective of transcendence (the Overman)?

The central issue in any interpretation is identifying the questions a philosopher was trying to answer. These last questions are not ones that can be addressed here, but I hope I have said enough to indicate why I think they are the sorts of questions Nietzsche was trying to answer, that his measuring himself against the tradition of the French moralists naturally and internally leads us to issues like these. At least one firm conclusion follows from all this: if we must give Nietzsche a label, "philosopher of the will" has for too long been a misleading and hasty characterization. Like his other great hero and enemy, he might claim, like Socrates, to know only one thing beyond his own ignorance—something about the mysteries of human eros.

References

Acampora, Christa Davis. Forthcoming. "Das Thun ist Alles." Comments on *Nietzsche: Moraliste français* at APA Author Meets Critics session, Dec. 2007.

Anderson, Lanier. Forthcoming. "Love and the Moral Psychology and the Hegelian Nietzsche." Comments on *Nietzsche: Moraliste français* at APA Author Meets Critics session, Dec. 2007.

Berry, Jessica N. 2004. "The Pyrrhonian Revival in Montaigne and Nietzsche." *Journal of the History of Ideas* 65:407–514.

Bittner, Rüdiger. 1994. "Ressentiment." In Schacht 1994, 127–38.

Brandom, Robert. 1994. *Making It Explicit: Reasoning, Representing, and Discursive Commitment.* Cambridge, MA: Harvard University Press.

Brobjer, Thomas. 2008. *Nietzsche's Philosophical Context: An Intellectual Biography.* Urbana: University of Illinois Press.

Brusotti, Marco. 1997a. *Die Leidenschaft der Ekenntnis: Philosopische und ästhetische Lebensgestaltung bei Nietzsche von Mogenröte bis Also sprach Zarathustra.* Berlin: de Gruyter.

———. 1997b. "Erkenntnis als Passion: Nietzsches Denkweg zwischen Morgenröte und der Fröhliche Wissenschaft." *Nietzsche-Studien* 26:199–225.

Carlyle, Thomas. 1849. "Occasional Discourse on the Negro Question." *Fraser's Magazine for Town and Country* (London), vol. 40.

Clark, Maudemarie. 1983. "Nietzsche's Doctrines of the Will to Power." *Nietzsche-Studien* 12:458–68.

Conant, J. Forthcoming. "Remarks on Pippin for APA Session." Comments on *Nietzsche: Moraliste français* at APA Author Meets Critics session, Dec. 2007.

Devereux, Georges. 1983. *Baubo, la vulve mythique*. Paris: J.-C. Goedfroy.

Donnellan, Brendan. 1982. *Nietzsche and the French Moralists*. Bonn: Bouvier.

Emerson, Ralph Waldo. 1970. *The Journals and Miscellaneous Notebooks*. Vol. 8, *1841–1843*. Ed. William Gilman and J. E. Parsons. Cambridge, MA: Belknap Press.

———. 1972 . *The Early Lectures*. Vol. 3, *1838–1842*. Ed. Robert E. Spiller and Wallace E. Williams. Cambridge, MA: Belknap Press.

Frankfurt, Harry G. 1988. *The Importance of What We Care About*. Cambridge: Cambridge University Press.

———. 1999. *Necessity, Volition, and Love*. Cambridge: Cambridge University Press.

Freud, S. 1963. "Mourning and Melancholia." In *General Psychological Theory*, ed. Philip Rieff. New York: Collier.

Gemes, Kenneth. 2006. "Nietzsche on Free Will, Autonomy, and the Sovereign Individual." *Proceedings of the Aristotelian Society*, supplementary vol. 80: 339–57.

Geuss, Raymond. 1999. "Nietzsche and Morality." In *Morality, Culture and History: Essays on German Philosophy*. Cambridge: Cambridge University Press.

Gray, Floyd. 1958. *Le Style de Montaigne*. Paris: Nizet.

Haugeland, John. 2000. *Having Thought: Essays in the Metaphysics of Mind*. Cambridge, MA: Harvard University Press.

Heftrich, Eckart. 1962. *Nietzsches Philosophie: Identität vom Welt und Nichts*. Frankfurt a.M.: Klostermann.

Heidegger, M. 1961. Nietzsche. Vols. 1 and 2. Pfullingen: Neske.

———. 1975ff. *Gesamtausgabe*. Frankfurt a.M.: Klostermann.

Kaufmann, Walter. 1968. *Nietzsche: Philosopher, Psychologist, Anti-Christ*. New York: Meridien Books.

———. 1974. "Translator's Introduction." *"The Gay Science," by Friedrich Nietzsche*. New York: Vintage.

Kofman, Sarah. 1972. *Nietzsche et la métaphore*. Paris: Paylot.

———. 1986. *Nietzsche et la scène philosophique*. Paris: Édition Galilée.

Landy, Joshua. 2004. *Philosophy as Fiction: Self, Deception and Knowledge in Proust*. Oxford: Oxford University Press.

Lear, J. 1990. *Love and Its Place in Nature*. New York: Farrar, Straus, and Giroux.

Lear, Jonathan. 2006. *Radical Hope: Ethics in the Face of Cultural Devastation*. Cambridge, MA: Harvard University Press, 2006.

Meier, Heinrich. 2003. *Das theologisch-politische Problem: Zum Thema von Leo Strauss*. Stuttgart: Metzler.

Molner, David. 1993. "The Influence of Montaigne on Nietzsche." *Nietzsche-Studien* 22:80–93.

Montaigne, Michel de. 1962. *Œuvres completes*. Ed. Maurice Rat. Paris: Gallimard.

———. 2002. *Les essais*. Ed. Claude Pinganaud. Paris: Arléa.

Pascal, Blaise. 1963. *Œuvres completes*. Edition and notes by Louis Fuma. Paris: Seuil.

Pippin, Robert. 1981. *Kant's Theory of Form*. New Haven, CT: Yale University Press.

———. 1988. "Irony and Affirmation in Nietzsche's *Thus Spoke Zarathustra*." In *Nietzsche's New Seas: Explorations in Philosophy, Aesthetics, and Politics*, ed. Michael Allen Gillespie and Tracy Strong. Chicago: University of Chicago Press.

———. 1997. *Idealism as Modernism: Hegelian Variations*. Cambridge: Cambridge University Press.

———. 1999a. *Modernism as a Philosophical Problem: On the Dissatisfactions of European High Culture*. 2nd ed. Oxford: Blackwell.

———. 1999b. "Nietzsche and the Melancholy of Modernity." *Social Research* 66 (2): 495–519.

———. 2000a. "Deceit, Desire, and Democracy: Nietzsche on Modern Eros." *International Studies in Philosophy* 32 (3): 63–70.

———. 2000b. "Gay Science and Corporeal Knowledge." *Nietzsche-Studien* 29:136–52.

———. 2000c. "What Is the Question for Which Hegel's 'Theory of Recognition' Is the Answer?" *European Journal of Philosophy* 8 (2): 155–72.

———. 2006. "Introduction" to *Thus Spoke Zarathustra*. Ed. with Adrian del Caro. Cambridge: Cambridge University Press.

———. 2008a. *Hegel's Practical Philosophy: Rational Agency as Ethical Life*. Cambridge: Cambridge University Press.

———. 2008b. Review of *The Affirmation of Life*, by Bernard Reginster. *Philosophy and Phenomenological Research* 77 (1): 281–91.

———. Forthcoming. *American Myth and Hollywood Westerns: The Importance of Howard Hawks and John Ford for Political Philosophy*. New Haven, CT: Yale University Press.

Poellner, Peter. 2004. "Self-Deception, Consciousness and Value." *Journal of Consciousness Studies* 11 (10–11): 45–65.

———. 2009. "Nietzschean Freedom." In *Nietzsche on Freedom and Autonomy*, ed. Kenneth Gemes and Simon May, 151–80. Oxford: Oxford University Press.

Prauss, Gerold. 1971. *Erscheinung bei Kant*. Berlin: de Gruyter.

Reginster, Bernard. 2006. *The Affirmation of Life: Nietzsche on the Overcoming of Nihilism*. Cambridge, MA: Harvard University Press.

Schacht, R. ed. 1994. *Nietzsche, Genealogy, Morality: Essays on Nietzsche's "On the Genealogy of Morals."* Berkeley: University of California Press.

Searle, John. 2001. *Rationality in Action*. Cambridge, MA: MIT Press.

Taylor, Charles. 1975. *Hegel*. Cambridge: Cambridge University Press.

———. 1985a. "Hegel's Philosophy of Mind." In Taylor 1985b, 77–96.

———. 1985b. *Human Agency and Language: Philosophical Papers*. Vol. 1. Cambridge: Cambridge University Press.

———. 1985c. "What Is Human Agency?" In Taylor 1985b, 15–44.

Vivarelli, Vivetta. 1994. "Montaigne und der freie Geist." *Nietzsche-Studien* 23: 79–101.

Walker, Barbara G. 1988. *The Woman's Dictionary of Symbols and Sacred Objects*. San Francisco: Harper and Row.

Williams, Bernard. 1985. *Ethics and the Limits of Philosophy*. Cambridge, MA: Harvard University Press.

——. 1994. "Nietzsche's Minimalist Moral Psychology." In Schacht 1994, 237–47.

Williams, W. D. 1952. *Nietzsche and the French*. Oxford: Blackwell.

Index

individuality, 61–62, 122

inner vs. outer states, 72n5, 78–79, 81, 91–93, 94–96, 100

inseparability thesis, 3, 46–47, 56–57, 59, 68, 70–84, 92, 99–101, 110

instinct(s), 40–41; consciousness contrasted with, 86–93, 96, 100; knowledge vs., 39–40; of philosophers, 6n9; problem of, 58

intentionality, 24–25, 72, 75, 76n8, 77–79, 88–90, 94, 119–20

interpretation: bias in, 103; culture's role in, 58, 102; of deed, 80, 82–84; of desire, 88–90; errors in, 100; of mastery, 118; of meaning of deed, 99–100, 104; need for, 64; psychological, 24–25, 68–69, 87, 90–93; of self-creation, 109–11; self-knowledge as, 101; of suffering, 61–62, 100; of tradition, 5–6

judgment(s), 40, 83, 86, 93–94, 100. *See also* value(s)

justice, 35–38, 40, 119n12. *See also* conscience, intellectual

Kant, Immanuel, 25n5, 31n16, 38, 43, 61, 89, 106

knowledge: desire for, 37–38, 57, 63; embodiment of, 39–41; modernity and, 39–40; nihilism and, 52; self-desire for, 14–20; truth and, 42–43, 53n15

Kofman, Sarah, xv, 47n2

Kritische Studienausgabe, xiv, 8n14

La Fontaine, Jean de, 96

Lang, Albert, 8n12

La Rochefoucauld, François, 8, 10, 14, 23, 49, 68

"last men," 30, 32, 37, 50–51, 52, 69–70, 113

Lebensphilosophien, xvin4

lies, 44, 52, 90, 92–93, 94. *See also* self-deceit

life: attachment as condition of, 15, 44, 51; Hegelian view of, 122–23; illusion necessary for, 31, 64, 117n10; perspective of, 3n3, 12, 13n27, 14, 19, 40–41, 54–57, 120; philosophy as condition of, 16–17, 41; requirements of, 35, 44; secret as revealed to Zarathustra, 117; as will to power, 5, 35; Zarathustra's definition of, 3n3

"lightning/flash" image, xvii, 71–72, 74, 76–77, 92

love: commitment and, 27; illusion necessary for, 31; impossibility of teaching, 57; of mankind, 13; Montaigne's views on, 123; philosophy as, 16–17; possession and, 17–18, 19n29; in Provençal lyric poetry, 35, 41; psychology of, 15, 21; unrequited, 38; "way of the lover" discussion, 114–15. *See also* desire; eros

lovers, clumsy, 13–14, 15, 16, 18, 19, 46

"madman" image, 33n20, 47–51, 52

Magritte, René, 43

Marx, Karl, 61

masters: achievement of, 118; determinism and, 81; enemies needed by, 82; ideals of, 26; morality, 26, 107; necessity of, 117–18; strength of, 70–72, 75–76, 118–19. *See also* slave revolt

Matthew, Gospel of, 13

melancholy, 33n20, 48n5, 49–50, 54, 65, 68

Melville, Herman, 29

metaphors. *See* images

metaphysics, metaphysicians, 72, 105; anti-Cartesian opposition to, 77; end of, 47–49; Kant's views on, 38; moralists contrasted with, 11, 19n30; Nietzsche and, xiii, xv, 84, 85, 97, 110, 118; problem of freedom in, 106; replacement by psychology, 1–2, 4–9

misogyny, 14